# SUCCESS
## IS
# A CHOICE

ALSO BY RICK PITINO

*Born To Coach*
*Full Court Pressure*

# SUCCESS
## IS
# A CHOICE

## TEN STEPS TO
## OVERACHIEVING
## IN BUSINESS AND LIFE

# RICK PITINO

## with BILL REYNOLDS

BROADWAY BOOKS • NEW YORK

**BROADWAY**

Broadway Books titles may be purchased for business or promotional use or for special sales. For information, please write to: Special Markets Department, Bantam Doubleday Dell Publishing Group, Inc., 1540 Broadway, New York, NY 10036. BROADWAY BOOKS and its logo, a letter B bisected on the diagonal, are trademarks of Broadway Books, a division of Bantam Doubleday Dell Publishing Group, Inc.

*Designed by Stanley S. Drate/Folio Graphics Co., Inc.*

Library of Congress Cataloging-in-Publication Data

Pitino, Rick.
    Success is a choice : ten steps to overachieving in business and
life / by Rick Pitino with Bill Reynolds.—1st ed.
      p.  cm.
    ISBN 0-553-06668-4 (hardcover)
    1. Success—Psychological aspects.  I. Reynolds, Bill,
1945–  .
  II. Title.
 BF637.S8P57  1997
158.1—dc21                                97-2298
                                                    CIP

97  98  99  00  01  10

For Sal Pitino and Bill Minardi Sr., two humble men who possessed the work ethic of a champion. Special people travel to special places. I look up every day and think of you.

—RICK PITINO

To my sister Polly, whose persistence in the face of great adversity is a daily inspiration.

—BILL REYNOLDS

# CONTENTS

# CONTENTS

# ACKNOWLEDGMENTS

Many people go into the making of a book, and at the risk of leaving some people out, we would like to publicly thank a few special ones.

David Vigliano, our literary agent who first brought us together on a book nearly ten years ago, believed in this idea from the beginning and pushed to make it a reality. John Sterling of Broadway Books initially saw the potential of the project, and his vision of what the book should be was a constant and invaluable guide. Suzanne Oaks shepherded this book through all the stages with great skill and matching commitment, especially in the last month against tight deadlines. It couldn't have gotten done without her.

They all have our enduring thanks.

Thanks also to Tom Wallace, for his research and help; Tom Healy, for his friendship and the use of his house in Saratoga, New York, where much of the book was shaped in the summer of 1996; and Ken "Jersey Red" Ford for his constant support.

Most of all, this book never could have been written without the many loyal assistant coaches and players over the years at Boston University, Providence College, the New York Knicks, and the University of Kentucky. Without their great work ethic, sacrifice, and commitment—and their ability to let nothing hinder their pursuit of their dreams—there would not be a book.

—RICK PITINO and BILL REYNOLDS

# DESERVING VICTORY

Winston Churchill's rallying cry for the British people during WW II was simple and succinct: hoping and praying for victory was fine, but deserving it was what really mattered.

What does it mean to "deserve victory"?

According to Churchill, victory comes only to those who work long and hard, who are willing to pay the price in blood, sweat, and tears. Hard work is also the basic building block of every kind of achievement: Without it, everything else is pointless. You can start with a dream or an idea or a goal, but before any of your hopes can be realized, you truly must deserve your success. This may sound old-fashioned in this age of instant gratification, but from the Sistine Chapel to the first transcontinental railroad to today's space shuttle, there's no mystery as to how these things of wonder were created. They were created by people who worked incredibly hard over a long period of time.

If you look closely at all great organizations, all great teams, all great people, the one common denominator that runs through them is a second-to-none work ethic. The intense effort to achieve is always there. This is the one given if you want to be successful. When it comes to work ethic there can be no compromises. Any other promise of achievement is fool's gold.

We can see the evidence of fool's gold around us every day. It's the people looking for the quick fix. The easy way to lose weight. The no-pain way to have a better body. The instant way to get rich. The easy, no-assembly-required way to feel better about yourself, as if all you have to do is follow some simple directions and your problems will disappear like frost in the noonday sun.

But shortcuts fail.

The bottom line: Nothing meaningful or lasting comes without working hard at it, whether it's in your own life or with people you're trying to influence.

Take our basketball program at the University of Kentucky: We see ourselves as the hardest-working team in America. That is our standard, the yardstick by which we measure ourselves. We try to live up to it every day.

Are we the hardest-working team in America?

Who knows?

And who cares.

The important thing is we believe it. That's our edge. In close games, when the pressure intensifies and the margin between who wins and who loses can be as thin as an eggshell, we believe that all our hard work, all the long hours, and all the perspiration will enable us to come out on top. Why? Because we deserve it. We deserve our victory; we feel we've swatted more blood than our opponents and will earn it the old-fashioned way.

In my years of coaching I have worked with many players and seen a variety of attitude problems. Some players were selfish. Some doubted what we were trying to do. Some weren't as committed to the team concept as they should have been. I can live with all that. What I can't live with is a player who won't work hard. If players are willing to give the effort, they have no problem with me.

And you know what?

What's true on the basketball court is true in business and in life. You want to succeed? Okay, then succeed. Deserve it. How? Outwork everybody in sight. Sweat the small stuff. Sweat the big stuff. Go the extra mile. But whatever it takes, put your heart and soul into everything you do. Leave it all out on the court.

But that won't happen unless you choose to make it happen. Success is not a lucky break. It is not a divine right. It is not an accident of birth.

Success is a choice.

*   *   *

People ask me, why a motivational book, Rick?

Simple.

This is what I do.

It's what I've done for twenty-two years, ever since I graduated from the University of Massachusetts in 1974 and began to coach. I learned quickly that motivating people would be the most important responsibility of my career.

When I became a head coach at Boston University, I was just twenty-four years old. I was stepping into a program that hadn't had a winning season in years. I knew that if I didn't find a way to get the players I'd inherited to play appreciably better in a very short time, my dream of coaching was going to end in a small college gym somewhere. I immediately began reading about the coaching legends like Vince Lombardi and

John Wooden, looking for clues as to what had made them connect with their players, looking for anything that I could emulate and use as my own.

What I found had nothing to do with strategy but rather with how these great coaches motivated players to achieve victory. Very early on, I learned that I was simply unleashing the potential in the people I was coaching. I was motivating them not by intimidation but by showing them that it was their choice to win or lose. By giving them an "outside" perspective on who they were and how they presented themselves to the rest of the team and everyone who watched them, I helped the players realize their strengths and weaknesses so that they could figure out how they were going to improve.

I have no illusions about myself as a basketball coach. I wouldn't dare say that I know more about basketball than other coaches or that I have a better strategy. I know that many other coaches work just as hard as I do, put in as many long hours, are just as dedicated. I learned long ago that coaches can be successful using many different philosophies and that there is no sure-fire method to success.

I have been successful as a coach because I've been able to get people to do things they didn't think they were capable of doing.

An example:

When I became the coach of Providence College in the spring of 1985, I was inheriting a program that had been languishing near the bottom of the very competitive Big East Conference ever since the conference began in 1979. I had been an assistant coach with the New York Knicks at the time, and there were people who warned me that the Providence job was a graveyard for coaches.

In one of my first meetings with the team, I listed four categories on the blackboard: basketball, school, work ethic, family. The four supposedly most important parts of my new players' lives.

"How many of you want to be professional basketball players someday?" I asked.

Virtually every hand in the room went up.

"Well, since you've had a losing season last year and there is no one here in this room who averaged at least ten points a game last year, it's obvious you are not a success in the basketball part of your lives," I said, erasing one quarter of the blackboard. "And since I've seen your grade point averages, it's also obvious you aren't successful in school either."

The room was silent as I erased another quarter of the blackboard. Then I turned to the trainer and asked him how many players had been in the gym every day since the season ended. I wanted to know how many had been working on their games.

"No one, Coach," the trainer said.

'So it's obvious you don't work hard either," I said, erasing another quarter of the blackboard.

Then I started raising my voice.

"Let's see," I said. "You aren't successful in basketball, you aren't successful in school, and you don't work hard. What's left?"

I paused for emphasis.

"Well, hopefully, you're a close team," I finally said. "Hopefully, you care about each other."

"Oh, we do, Coach," said a player named Harold Starks. "We're a close team."

I pretended to think for a minute.

"Okay, Harold, how many brothers does Steve Wright have?"

Starks slowly shook his head.

"What does Billy Donovan's father do for a living?"

Harold now looked like a deer stuck in the headlights.

"So you really don't know anything about each other, do you?" I asked.

No one spoke.

I made each player stand up and talk about himself and his family. Then something wonderful happened. What had been twelve individuals suddenly had become a cohesive unit. The makings of a team.

Twenty-two months later that collection of individuals—now a team—would be in the Final Four, the greatest stage in all of college basketball. The message I tried to communicate had started the players on the road to becoming a cohesive, hardworking group of people whose change in attitude about themselves as individuals had made all the difference.

Fiery speeches and locker-room dramatics can be effective and certainly have their place, but you have to remember that their message is essentially short-lived. True motivation must go way beyond that; it must make people understand the process required to achieve success. In this case, that message was the bonding of individuals sharing the same dreams and goals.

But the most important thing I learned was that the keys to performing well—on or off the court—were the same for all of us. Whether it's a college athlete playing at a level he never thought he could, or a salesperson striving to break records, or anyone taking more control of his or her life, the formula is the same.

Hard work and togetherness help us to soar to the next level.

Success means different things to different people. For some, it's money. For some, it's power. For others, it's the respect of their peers, or it's self-satisfaction. For many, it's the desire to have better relationships with the people in their lives.

Everyone wants to succeed, no question about that. Even people who are the most cynical and pessimistic. We all want to be more productive. We all want to feel as though we are reaching our full potential. We all want to feel as though we're controlling our destiny, that we're not being controlled by it.

I have often been approached to do a motivational book. Although I was convinced that I could tell people the correct way to go about achieving goals, I had always refused. Over the past several years, I have witnessed many rags-to-riches stories and have been around so many athletes who have gone on to accomplish things that even they once thought were impossible. Yet I have also seen promising people get swept up by victory and fall back into laziness and complacency. I have seen people face tough times and give up, shielding themselves with excuses you will never hear from people who are true lifelong winners. It is the knowledge I've gained from watching both these groups that makes me feel that I'm now ready to share what I've learned. You see, from these experiences and various efforts, it has been proven to me over and over that success is truly a choice for people, and there is a formula for a lifetime of successful behavior.

That can't be stressed enough.

We want to reach our dreams but often lack the proper direction necessary to see those dreams come true. We seem to be forever floundering without knowing why, our good intentions wasted, all but programmed for failure.

We all want to be recognized for what we do.

We all want to feel we have value.

The problem is that many of us don't know how to get there.

Most of us, of course, don't have a coach following us

around in our lives to make sure we're on track. I hope that this book will be your own personal "coach" or tool for success.

It will show you how to create discipline in your life, establish a work ethic, create a sense of self-esteem in both yourself and others, learn how to fight through the inevitable adversity we all encounter in life, and be able to accomplish things you never dreamed possible.

All these goals are attainable, but each requires action and commitment.

It's up to you.

## WE NEED A PLAN OF ATTACK

A lot of young people come in to see me after finishing four years of college. I sit them down and ask, "What do you want to do with your life?"

Many of them give me a blank stare and then invariably say, "I don't know."

"I don't know" is the classic sign of the underachiever. They don't know because they haven't thought about it. Or, if they have thought about it, it's in fuzzy, unfocused terms. Or else they have dreams but no idea how to achieve them. The point is that there's no plan, no vision of what's necessary to get from the starting point to the finish line. No discipline.

Such people have not established a motive. Nor have they thought about establishing one. However, that doesn't mean that a motive can't change completely or be altered to adjust to events or circumstances in life. But first you must establish the direction you are heading in, and there's only one way to do that. That's by planning.

Discipline can be many things. It can be punishment. It can be hard work.

To me, it's a code of conduct, an organized plan of attack.

Discipline is our plan, our awareness of where we are starting from and what road to take to arrive at our destination. Without a plan we end up going in many different directions, lost in some personal maze, some labyrinth that just takes us around and around, wasting time and energy and distracts us from our goals. Without a plan we keep covering old territory.

There's more to it than simply making the effort. The effort must be one with a purpose, a sense of direction. You must have a purpose, and that purpose is called motive. By creating this discipline and by combining it with organization and methods, you are leveraging this motive for positive results. You have no more doubts.

Why?

Because you have a strategy. Because you are dedicated to fulfilling it. Because you have paid the price to be successful.

## THE 10 STEPS

Okay, you want to succeed. You're willing to do everything possible to realize your dreams.

Where do you start?

With the 10 steps.

The steps in this book represent the plan of attack. They mark the various way stations on the road to being more successful. They constitute the process of achieving dramatically greater results, whether it's at your job, in a classroom, whether you're trying to improve at a sport or hobby, or any activity you're involved in. It makes no difference. The techniques are the same.

The 10 steps are based on the premise that any of us can

achieve things we never thought possible—because most of us constantly undersell ourselves. We are conditioned to think we can't do things. We are conditioned to settle for less. We are conditioned to think our dreams are always going to be out of reach. We are conditioned to think that it's always going to be other people who grab life's brass ring. We are conditioned to fail.

But we don't have to.

We don't have to underachieve. We don't have to see our dreams recede in the distance. We don't have to fail. We can better our performance. We can reach our potential. We can change our lives.

The key is the 10 steps, the actions and behaviors rooted in more than two decades of my experience with success, with failure, and with learning how people's commitment—including my own—to these techniques makes the difference.

Attitude. Action. Persistence. These are the fundamentals we have to master in order to stretch beyond what we know. It is that self-challenge that keeps us reaching out for something better—that vision of ourselves running at peak performance all the time, constantly raising the level of our play.

But, again, we have to choose to commit to these fundamentals. Or we will simply maintain the status quo.

It's up to you.

# STEP 1
## BUILD
## SELF-ESTEEM

O ur self-esteem is the value we put on ourselves. It's the person we see when we look in the mirror.

I learned a long time ago as a coach that you can expect great things from people who feel good about themselves. They can push themselves. They can set long-term goals. They have dreams that everyone expects to be fulfilled. People with high self-esteem are risk takers, but more important, they are achievers.

Conversely, people with low self-esteem are often unfocused and easily frustrated. They tend to be underachievers, complete with the package that is so characteristic of those kinds of people: lack of discipline, poor organizational skills, an inability to finish things, a sense of discontent, sensitivity to criticism, envy of others—an entire laundry list of negatives. Whether you're a coach, employee, or co-worker, it's difficult to work with people with low self-esteem, because they tend to be emotionally fragile and conditioned for failure.

These negatives surrounding low self-esteem can sabo-tage us. If you become a victim of this condition, every other step in this book becomes meaningless.

It's the same with any organization or team. I've learned that when my team is leading at half-time I can be tough on them and demanding, for the simple reason that if the players feel good about themselves, they are better able to handle crit-icism and added expectations.

Yet when one of my teams is doing poorly at half-time, I am seldom critical because I know the players' collective es-teem is low and they are more fragile. At times like this they need support, need to feel better about themselves; their self-esteem must be built up.

So we cannot minimize the importance of self-esteem.

Without it, we become paralyzed. We are unable to move, to go into action.

I didn't always understand this.

When I was a young coach at Boston University I believed you treated everyone the same way. This was the philosophy of the times, and I was a product of that era. We all are prod-ucts of the values and attitudes that shaped us. When I was growing up, the coach was the absolute ruler. His words were chiseled in stone, his authority unquestioned. It was his way or the highway.

Even back then, I understood the importance of having a work ethic. I also understood that you had to have discipline to push yourself hard to deserve victory. A strong work ethic and discipline have been integral parts of my repertoire for the past two decades.

But I didn't understand the value of self-esteem. What I hadn't learned was that individuals with great self-esteem will do great things. They're the ones who make the big shots, the ones who want the ball in the closing seconds when the game is on the line and everything hangs in the balance. They're the ones you want in the workplace. They're the ones others count on to boost results and productivity when the company needs it most or who save an account in the waning moments by making a successful last-ditch effort.

Greatness can never be achieved unless we feel good about ourselves.

Mark Jackson is a perfect example of this.

Mark had been the eighteenth pick in the first round of the 1987 NBA draft. He was a local product who had been an excellent point guard in college at St. John's. Being the eighteenth pick in the draft means that seventeen clubs had already passed on the player we picked. The eighteenth pick is always a bit of a crap shoot. Still, there was much jubilation when the New York City product was chosen by the Knicks.

When I met with the staff to discuss our personnel, the mood suddenly turned somber when we began talking about Mark. There was anything but jubilation.

"What's the matter?" I asked.

"Well, Jackson's a little slow," one scout said.

"And he doesn't shoot it very well," said another.

There was a moment's hesitation.

"We also don't know if he can guard the quick guys in the league," said another voice.

I was stunned.

"Let's see," I said. "We just drafted a slow guy who can't shoot and who can't guard anyone either."

"It's the eighteenth pick, Rick," said one of the scouts. "That's what you get at eighteen."

I was devastated.

Mark was our guy, so I had to try to make it work out for us in a positive way. To begin with, I was determined to raise Mark's self-esteem because I knew that this was the only way he would believe for himself that he could perform better. He had to do what my players at Providence had done in order to get to the Final Four—establish a great work ethic, understand that they had to deserve success, and use that discipline to improve their self-esteem.

It became more complicated with Mark, because he held out for more money and was getting crucified in the New York tabloids, criticism that reminded him and everybody else of his weaknesses. So by the time he actually signed and came to camp, he had doubts about his ability to be successful in the NBA because the media kept bringing him down. He kept hearing he was too slow, that he didn't shoot well enough, that he couldn't defend. The same things my scouts had said to me.

Not surprisingly, Mark began to think he was going to fail. He looked around at the other rookies in the league who had been drafted ahead of him and began to envy them. Their games weren't being ripped apart in the press. Their abilities weren't being doubted.

Mark was falling into that all-too-familiar trap that so many people fall into. He was beginning to think everyone else had his act together, everyone, that is, except for him. It was as though he no longer felt he had the control to determine his own fate.

In order to reclaim the control he perceived he had lost, Mark had to exploit his strengths.

One of the first things I did was tell the rest of the team I thought Mark had a legitimate chance to be Rookie of the Year because he would flourish in our system. You could tell from the expression on everyone's face that they were not buying in to what I was saying. They laughed, and I could tell Mark was embarrassed. After all, eighteenth picks didn't become Rookie of the Year in the NBA, right?

But the strategy was to make Mark's strengths—his passing ability, his leadership, his charisma—as big as the sky and to shrink his weaknesses down to the size of a pea. Mark would focus on making himself unbeatable in his strengths, which I constantly reinforced to the team. If Mark thought the coach had confidence in him, he would rise to a level he never thought he could achieve.

I used to tell Mark that, outside of Magic Johnson, there wasn't a point guard in the league I wanted more than him. By making him feel good about himself, by raising his self-esteem, his doubts began to vanish, and he began to play great basketball for us. And that spring, in a ceremony at Tavern on the Green in Manhattan, less than a year after being chosen as the eighteenth pick in the draft, Mark Jackson was named the NBA's Rookie of the Year.

The thing to understand is that without a significant rise in his self-esteem none of this would have been possible. We must understand that Mark rose early, stayed late, and worked on all facets of his game that needed improving. He certainly paid his dues. For Mark was like most of us. As he began to feel better about himself, his performance started to improve. This, in turn, had a snowball effect. The more his performance improved, the better he felt about himself. He had begun a cycle of success that would give him the momentum he needed to clear every hurdle.

Mark became a classic example of what we talked about at the beginning of this chapter: You can expect great things from people who feel good about themselves.

Shortly afterward, I told Mark it was time to take his game to the next level. It was time to make the All-Star team.

He laughed.

"You know that's political," he said at first, thinking that he didn't have a real shot.

But because his self-esteem was now firmly established, he was able to raise his expectations and visualize himself getting picked. That next season Mark Jackson was named to play in the NBA All-Star Game.

Mark is also an example, however, of how fragile self-esteem can be. At the end of his second year, I left the Knicks to go to Kentucky. Soon after, I began reading in the New York papers that Mark was in trouble, that he didn't have our system anymore, a system that maximized his strengths and hid his weaknesses.

All of a sudden, I started reading about Mark's weaknesses again. And a strange thing happened. By the end of the next year Mark Jackson was no longer starting, and he was later traded to the Los Angeles Clippers. Though he's gone on to have a solid career and remain in the league, he's yet to return to the heights he did those first two years.

This should be a lesson to all of us. Extraordinary self-esteem produces extraordinary things.

Mark Jackson is the classic example of how we all need that powerful image of ourselves, that belief that we can accomplish great things, that magic elixir that we know as self-esteem. Without it, we are never going to reach our full potential.

None of us wants to be listless and floundering; none of us wants to feel as though life were controlling us. We don't like feeling powerless to do anything about it—like working on a mystery without any clues—feeling that we are miles away from reaching our true potential and that we have become little more than spectators watching life's parade go rushing by.

We all want to have more control over our lives. We all want to feel as though we're on the path to becoming more successful, complete with a road map to get us there. We all need a plan of attack and it starts with self-esteem.

Our plan of attack is the catalyst that jump-starts things and sets them in motion. Once we start to feel better about ourselves, we can then start to learn and practice the art of overachieving.

In real life, we don't have coaches or cheerleaders praising us to anyone who will listen. Real life isn't sports, although there are many similarities between the two.

So how do we, as individuals, raise our self-esteem?

First of all, let's begin by looking closely at that person in the mirror. You're not going to fool that person. He knows more about you than just how well groomed you are or what your hair and eyes look like. He knows exactly how hard you work, how organized you are, how good your plan of attack is. Much of self-esteem, in fact, is tied to being honest with yourself about whether you deserve victory. Therefore, don't try to fool the person in the mirror. You're only wasting time if you do.

You must establish a solid work ethic and a sound strategy in order to believe that you deserve success. Do that and it will make you feel better about yourself. It's all interrelated.

Consider the person who is overweight and unhappy about it. That person's self-esteem is almost certain to be low. How does he set about changing that situation?

The first thing he should do to conquer this unhappiness is establish the great work ethic. Set up a plan of attack, then put it in motion. This person might want to aim for something as simple as losing a few pounds over a couple of weeks.

The plan of attack creates the work ethic and the discipline to stay on a weight loss program, the attainable short-term goal. Reach the goal, and the message is sent to the overweight person that he now has a real plan and it's a successful one.

The message is that if you stick to that plan, you will start to control your weight problem rather than being controlled by it. Once you attain the short-term goal, you will inevitably start to feel better about yourself and your self-esteem will start to rise. The more it rises the more you can demand of yourself.

I have followed this basic approach with all my teams, through Boston University, Providence College, the New York Knicks, and now at Kentucky: Establish the work ethic, verbalize the goals, create the plan of attack, follow the proven methods, and very soon your esteem will start to rise as fast as Michael Jordan exploding to the rim.

Once you've created a work ethic second to none, and you've learned to motivate yourself, you look in the mirror and you see someone different. And it has nothing to do with appearances.

You see someone of value, someone who is going to be more successful, someone who is going to win. Because you have worked for it. You now deserve it. And that's what self-esteem is all about.

So let's understand that the power of self-esteem is the most important determining factor in reaching our potential. Before we can upgrade our skills and fundamentals, before we truly can start to achieve, we must believe that our value is worth improving. We must believe that our actions will make this possible.

## YOU'RE IN CONTROL

When I became the coach of Providence College in the spring of 1985, one of the players I inherited was Billy Donovan, a baby-faced kid who looked like the Pillsbury Doughboy. Billy already had spent two years at Providence without any basketball success. He was called too small, too slow, over-matched to play in a league as competitive as the Big East.

One of the first things he did was to come into my office and tell me that he wanted to transfer. He wanted to go to a school where he felt he could make more of an impact. He just didn't think he could play at this level. I told him I would help him switch schools if he felt that way, and I did try. But you know what? No one wanted him. So I told him that as long as he liked Providence, both academically and socially, why not give the team one more try?

But with an asterisk.

He had to lose thirty pounds. He had to get in the best shape of his life. In short, he had to start deserving victory.

He also had to understand the obstacles he had erected that stood in the way of his success. I asked him how persistent he was when it came to achieving his goals. He answered that he had a great love for the game and was willing to do whatever it took to make him a better player.

"If that's the case," I asked, "why are you thirty pounds more than you should be?"

Billy's excuse for being in such poor physical condition for a college athlete was that there were better guards ahead of him in the Providence program, and thus he didn't get much playing time.

Although Billy didn't realize it, he was transferring the blame for his failure to someone else, in this instance his former coach. Since Billy said he was out of shape because of a lack of playing time, and because coaches determine playing time, what he really was telling me was that it was the coach's fault. He had made his former coach the scapegoat, thus absolving himself from blame.

I had set the trap and Billy had fallen right into it. It was classic nonachiever behavior. Nonachievers create alibis for themselves. Nonachievers always blame someone else. It's never their fault that they're not achieving; it's always someone else's fault.

Billy considered himself to be a very self-motivated person, but he didn't know what that meant. I told Billy that truly self-motivated people are always knocking on the door to perform, and that the only way to seize the moment is to be ready when that moment arrives. I told him that I didn't want to hear any more reasons why he had failed. Then I sat down with him and laid out a list of ways for him to improve as a basketball player.

We had established the motive and turned his methods into action.

When he returned that fall, he was a different person. Lighter. Quicker. More confident as a player.

It was apparent that he had established a great work ethic. His being in great shape was a testimony to that.

It also was clear that he felt better about himself, that when he looked in the mirror now he was starting to see a Big East basketball player stare back, not someone who figured he was playing in an environment in which it was too competitive for him to succeed.

In fact, he looked so different I made him pose for the cover of our game program. I dressed him as a cowboy with full apparel—hat, boots, and two six-guns. He was mortified, but we made him do it anyway. From them on, Billy took on a new persona; we called him "Billy the Kid," and he would soon become "the fastest gun in the East." He became the cornerstone of our new era at Providence.

Well, by the time he graduated two years later Billy Donovan had become an All Big East player. He was the leading scorer on a team that went to the Final Four in 1987 and was a second round draft choice of the Utah Jazz. He was no longer the pudgy teenager he had been two years earlier. He was "Billy the Kid," one of the top point guards in the country.

Now when he looked into the mirror someone of value stared back. His self-esteem was sky high. He had learned to minimize his weaknesses and believe in his strengths. He had established the great work ethic, had devised a plan of attack, had begun to see the fruits of his labor, and had seen his self-esteem mushroom.

The result?

A totally different player than he'd been two years earlier.

What Billy Donovan learned transcends basketball and provides lessons we all can use in our daily lives.

He realized that he had more control over his life than he previously thought, that it wasn't just lucky breaks that made people achieve more than he did. Now, with his work ethic and elevated self-esteem, he could forge his own destiny. The "good fortune" he created was all directly tied to his work ethic.

That is one of the most important lessons we can learn.

It's easy to say that people who achieve more than we do are handed their victories on a silver platter. It's easy to dismiss their accomplishments and ignore their hard work. Underachiever mentality is about making excuses. Other people are lucky. Other people get the breaks, we don't. Other people get promotions because the boss likes them.

We can find many reasons to justify to ourselves why we are failing.

► I didn't go to the right school.

► The marketplace is too competitive.

▶ My job's too tough.

▶ There are no really good jobs anyway.

▶ I have too many responsibilities.

▶ It's all about contacts anyway, and I don't have any.

Ever hear any of these?

Ever use any yourself?

Odds are you have, because they are the perennials. At one time or another we all use them.

They are the built-in excuses, the reasons we use to make ourselves feel better. They are easy to conjure up and constitute the classic refrain of defeat.

This is the mentality of underachievers. The mentality that Billy Donovan had to rid himself of before he could start being more successful. The mentality that we all must break or else we'll look back and see our life as one big excuse.

The other major alibi for underachievement is blaming others for our failures, just as Billy Donovan indirectly blamed his former coach in his first meeting with me.

We do this all the time. The boss doesn't like me. My wife doesn't understand me. My co-workers don't understand the pressures on me. My teammates are jealous.

In other words, it's always someone else's fault. Someone else always shares part of the blame.

When Billy eventually realized his malaise was his fault—his and his alone—he had made a significant discovery. When he eventually understood that he controlled what happened to him, he began to feel empowered. That's a wonderful feeling. It tells us we don't have to depend on others. We don't have to be burdened by others' perceptions of us, whether right or wrong. It tells us our success or failure is up to us. We are the captains of our ship. We determine our own destiny.

For the truth is, we control our life. We control how lucky we are. We create our fortune with our effort.

We alone have the power.

## FIND YOUR ROLE IN THE GAME

When you're underachieving it's easy to think everyone else has the secret except you. You look around at successful people and think they have everything going for them; their lives are always as smooth and easy as a summer afternoon at the beach.

The reality is, though, we all have frustrations and failures. Even the people who, on the surface, appear as if they don't.

In the summer of 1987 I became the coach of the New York Knicks. I was thirty-four years old; and because I'd been born in New York City and always had been a great Knicks fan, becoming their coach was a dream come true.

But I quickly found out that it was all more complicated than that.

When I wanted to bring to the Knicks the same full-court trapping pressing style of play I had used in college, the media quickly jumped all over me. They said it would never work in the NBA, that the season was too long, there were too many games, and the players simply would not exert the kind of energy on a nightly basis that was essential if the style were to be successful. It seemed to me as if almost every day the New York papers said that our style of play would never work.

Even Al Bianchi, the Knicks' general manager and my boss, had his doubts, which certainly didn't make me feel real comfortable or secure in my job.

So here was a job that on the surface was supposed to be my dream but in actuality had quickly become very different.

Eventually, it started bothering me.

Not that I ever thought they were right. But what if they were half-right? What if 50 percent of what they said came true? For the first time I started to question myself. I always have been a very confident person, but all the daily sniping and questioning was taking its toll.

This went on throughout much of the season. Even when we started winning there were still doubters who said our style would eventually burn the players out. In fact, it wasn't until the last game of the regular season that I began to feel better. That was the night we qualified for the playoffs, the first time in years the Knicks had made it that far. The next day *New York Newsday* ran a headline that said "Vindicated."

But I learned a valuable lesson. I learned that you can't doubt yourself, that you have to maintain confidence that you are fulfilling the role you've staked out for yourself. My job wasn't to go to New York and do what everyone else had done. My role was to get in there and build a winner and not occupy my time with critics and second-guessers.

That's not to say you can't tinker with your plan or always try to make it better. You might very well find your plan to be faulty and have to adjust it, which we did my second year with the Knicks when we modified our style a bit, using our press in spots and not as a steady diet.

The point is, you have to be a risk-taker. You must be willing to take chances, to put yourself on the line, to throw yourself into the middle of activity. Even at the cost of people questioning you and doubting you.

Underachievers frequently don't understand their role in things.

They either don't know where they fit or they are unwilling to perform the role that's assigned to them.

Many people nowadays, in this age of instant gratification, don't have patience. They want everything to happen now. Instant this, instant that, instant success. They don't understand the value of patience, of waiting your turn, of being ready when the proper time comes.

When we set out to transform our lives, there should be no time limit. We are looking for change over the long haul, change that is going to be with us for the rest of our lives. In order to make this change, we must be aware of our strengths and weaknesses, because we all have them. The key is not only knowing which ones are which but also knowing how to manage them. I learned this by observing athletes, all of whom have to cope with their strengths and liabilities. But it's not just athletes; we all have to do this. Our job is to define a role for ourselves that maximizes our strengths and minimizes our weaknesses.

So many times in life we see people who don't understand this. It's the guy at the party who is always trying to be funny, but isn't. The person trying to be a salesman who has neither the personality nor the temperament to sell food to a starving man. Young people who wear ridiculous clothes simply because of peer pressure. These are people who don't understand what they should and shouldn't be doing.

It happens in sports all the time.

So many players refuse to believe they have any weaknesses at all. When you point them out, they respond, "You're wrong. I can do that." They often begin to focus all their efforts proving everyone wrong, and in so doing they move away from their strengths.

Two years ago, I coached a young man named Rodrick Rhodes, who had come to Kentucky as a celebrated prep All-American from St. Anthony's High School in Jersey City, New Jersey. Now, Rodrick is a wonderful person, but he became convinced that to become a pro he had to prove he could shoot the basketball with range. No matter that he was a great slasher and had a great post-up game. No matter that he could get to the foul line consistently or hit the fifteen-foot shot. That wasn't enough anymore. He began focusing on the people who told him he had to show the NBA scouts he could make perimeter shots. He tuned out common sense and wasted his time and energy trying to fulfill a role he never could play. As a result, his game suffered.

How many prize fighters have we seen who know that the only way they can win the fight is to elude their opponent, to dance and jab and stay away from them? Then what do they do? They end up going toe-to-toe trying to show everyone how tough they are. They try to show everyone they don't have any weaknesses.

That strategy is a losing one.

We have to be honest with ourselves about how we stack up against everyone else. Not everyone can be quarterback, not everyone can be the superstar of a team. The reality is that we're living and working in a world with a lot of people with different talents and skills. We have to position ourselves to be unique so that we can be the best in our area of expertise. If we try to be the best in an area we're only mediocre in, we're setting ourselves up for a self-esteem disaster.

We will start to believe we are good at nothing.

But if we leverage a skill we already have, we can corner the market in that area. However, we must identify our weaknesses and allow a certain amount of time in our daily routine to turn those weaknesses into future strengths.

Dennis Rodman of the Chicago Bulls has been smart about this. Forget for a moment Rodman's flamboyance and eccentricities and attitude. As a basketball player, he realizes that rebounding the basketball is his strength, and everything he does on the court is geared to that. We too must create a role for ourselves that elicits our confidence. This is what makes us stand tall as we face dramatic change.

## IT'S NEVER TOO LATE TO CHANGE

Age is no criterion when it comes to changing your life.

In fact, it might be just the opposite.

The older we get, the more we must change.

Change is what keeps us fresh and innovative. Change is what keeps us from getting stale and stuck in a rut. Change is what keeps us young.

This is especially true in today's business climate, where companies are streamlining and downsizing. You simply cannot use age as an excuse. You cannot say you're too old to change, too set in your ways, too accustomed to what you're doing. They're not excuses anymore. You either adapt, or you will be left behind.

This is not easy.

When we are young it's easy to change and experiment with different things. When I was a young coach at Boston University I didn't have any experience, but I also didn't have many doubts either. I didn't know a lot of things, and my job was a little like going into my own laboratory every day to experiment. With no history of what worked and what didn't work for me, I tried new strategies, new drills, new exercises—anything that might teach me a better way to approach coaching and motivating the players. The energy of youth was my luxury.

The older we get the more set in our ways we become. We've found out what our comfort level is, and we all want to stay in it. We don't want to be risk takers anymore, because risk frightens us, and simply not changing seems so easy.

We must fight through this. We must look fear straight in

the eye and take it on. We must tell ourselves that we have too much talent, too much wisdom, too much value not to change. In today's economic climate we have no choice.

I believe that Jim O'Brien, who is on my staff at Kentucky, is one of the best assistant coaches in the country. But I almost didn't hire him three years ago because I thought that psychologically he was too "old," that he had lost the drive and passion that an assistant coach needs. He had worked for me with the New York Knicks and then had become the head coach at Dayton. He was an instant success until Dayton got into a too-difficult league, resulting in an unsuccessful team and things not working out for Jim.

Three years ago he was forty, and I thought he might have spent too many Saturday afternoons at the country club, that he wasn't going to get in the trenches anymore, like the younger assistant coaches do. That was my bias Jim had to overcome. But Jim told me that he couldn't wait to get down in the trenches again. So I hired him, and he's been an integral part of our success at Kentucky.

Yet he had to sell himself to me. He had to convince me he still had the same energy and desire that he'd had when he was younger.

Before he could do that, though, he'd had to convince himself he could resurrect the passion he had when he was younger. He had to convince himself that if he could summon drive and energy and then combine them with the wisdom he'd gained from all his coaching experience that he would still be a valuable commodity in coaching. I know what you're thinking. How can forty be old?

There is a conventional wisdom in coaching that once you've been a head coach you can't enthusiastically go back to being an assistant again and still have the same passion as before. Jim didn't buy into that. He didn't let his "old age" get in his way. He found a way to tap into his rather rare strength of experience and overcame his perceived weaknesses. He kept his self-esteem high. He was ready when opportunity came calling. He put himself in a climate where he could be successful. He reestablished a work ethic second to none with the eagerness of a person right out of college. And I'm thankful he did, because he played such an essential role in our championship season.

This is what we all must do.

We must realize that it's never too late to begin making changes that can transform our life.

## WE MUST DESERVE SELF-ESTEEM

Self-esteem comes with a catch, though.

We must deserve it.

Only when you have your plan of attack, you become organized, have discipline in your life, you're prepared to win— that's when you should start to give yourself some credit.

Only when you've proven that you deserve victory.

It's counterproductive to boost someone's self-esteem when that person doesn't deserve it.

That's the mistake many parents and teachers make. They try to constantly raise a child's self-esteem because self-esteem has become one of the big buzzwords in our culture, and they've been led to believe that first and foremost a child has to feel good about himself.

Let's examine the stereotype of the listless child in front of the TV set. A child who has unfocused goals, no discipline, no organization. Yet his parents tell him he's acting perfectly acceptably when he's sitting there staring blankly at the TV screen.

That's counterproductive, a blueprint for failure.

The parents who keep telling their young child he is one day going to conquer the world and do great things while that child is constantly watching TV without any purpose whatsoever is doing that child a disservice. They don't mean to. They are no doubt well intentioned. But they are leading that child to failure because they are building up hopes that are never going to be actualized.

The most realistic profession that child is headed for is couch potato, devoid of the skills that are going to help him reach his dreams. He is not worthy of being praised. He has done nothing to deserve being made to feel good about himself. Pretending he has is only self-delusion, and self-delusion will always come back to haunt you. Only when that child starts to deserve victory will that person in the mirror start to have some genuine value.

I remember a real-life story. After giving a speech on self-esteem, a horse-trainer friend of mine came up to me and told me how much he enjoyed the speech. He said that after listening to me he felt really good about himself and that it was going to make him a better trainer. He had a good feeling inside. Great things were going to happen. Now this is a man who has been successful. He'd moved from New York to Kentucky, and he's as talented as anyone in the game.

After listening to him tell me how he now had a new lease on life, I told him that that was only the beginning, that he had to deserve success. So, in essence, he was only half-right. I then went on to tell him that until he deserved that mood, it would evaporate in a short period of time. He questioned me, asking why I doubted him. I said, "Okay, now you have the belief. But that won't do you any good until you have the execution. Until you rise early, stay late, pay a bigger price. Until you do those things, genuine self-esteem is going to be an elusive goal."

I wasn't going to patronize him just because he's my friend. That wasn't going to help him fulfill his potential. We must stay away from patronization; it only builds mirages in people's lives. My friend, who had only been talking a good game, finally put his talk into action. The result? He set the Turfway Park record for most wins by a trainer and had the highest winning percentage in that track's history.

It's the same with all of us.

Many people believe that simply saying an affirmation over and over will make it a reality. But repeating "I will get a raise and a promotion by June" five times a day isn't going to make it happen.

If we keep telling ourselves we are going to be successful—or if we keep fantasizing it—but we don't do the necessary things to prepare ourselves to actually be more successful, then we are only deceiving ourselves. Just as that couch potato lying on the couch fantasizing about one day being a doctor is deceiving himself.

Only when we know we deserve it can we start to feel better about ourselves and arrive at genuine self-esteem. At that point our self-esteem has been earned and has significant value.

## WE ALL NEED TO BE VALUED

Now let's take a few minutes to examine how we can raise the self-esteem of someone else, whether that of a child, a co-worker, a loved one, or someone who you are leading in a volunteer activity. Again, it makes no difference. The techniques are the same.

To a young person, gratification means that you are successful. However, as we get older, we want the people we are teaching to be successful. That's the true wisdom that comes with maturity.

People are forever asking me if winning that national championship was the crowning point in my coaching career. I don't have the words to tell you how much pride I felt in being a part of something that was so wonderful, not only for our team and university but also for our state. We always were conscious of just how much the people of Kentucky deserved a national championship. So, of course, winning the title in 1996 was one of those truly magical moments both for myself and my family.

But in all honesty it wasn't any greater than the night of the NBA draft. I was working as an analyst for TNT, and there were four of my players getting drafted. I saw these young men who had worked so hard for me hugging their families. I saw how happy they were and how far they'd come from when they had first arrived as freshman, full of the same doubts and anxieties about the future that all freshmen have when they enter college.

That was the ultimate moment in my career.

I got more true satisfaction from that night than from anything I've ever done in basketball, because I knew that I had played a role in filling somebody's cup with so much joy.

Because what you eventually find out—when you're looking only for your own individual gratification—is that it's short lived. But when you have had a hand in someone else's success, it's that connection, that bond, that can last a lifetime.

In a sense it's the difference between talent and greatness. We all know what talent is. It's usually very demonstrable and is an individual action like an amazing three-pointer from across the court. But greatness is when you bring more to the table than just yourself. When you go to the table with greatness everyone eats better, not just you.

We see it in sports all the time.

The NBA is full of extremely talented players who never seem to win anything significant. Sometimes that's not their fault: They are merely victims of forces they can't control. But we all can think of talented players who never make anyone else around them better. They put up great numbers. They can be human highlight films, capable of wondrous athletic feats. But their teams don't win.

Compare them to the Magic Johnsons, the Larry Birds, the Michael Jordans. There really is no comparison. The one common denominator these three share is that their presence raises everyone else's performance level. That's what greatness is. And that's what great leaders are continually trying to do: make the people around them better.

We must never forget this.

Take the case of Anthony Epps, for example.

Anthony was the starting point guard on our national championship Kentucky team as a junior, our unsung hero. He was probably the least acclaimed of all our players coming into Kentucky, and even now everyone's always talking about how everyone else on our team is going to play professional basketball, whether it's Ron Mercer, Derek Anderson, or Jeff Sheppard. No one ever mentions Anthony Epps, because, quite frankly, people just don't talk about him as having the kind of athletic ability necessary to play in the NBA. Nor did he really think of himself as having the potential to one day be in the NBA, for the simple reason that no one ever mentioned him in that context, even though he had played such a main part in helping us win the national title.

So one day last spring I called him into the office.

"Do you know what the real shame of all this is?" I said

to Anthony. "Right now everyone's always talking about all the other guys as having a chance to one day play in the NBA and no one ever mentions you. How do you feel about that, Anthony?"

"Well, I guess I just don't have the skills to play at that level," he said.

"Let's take a look at your skills," I said. "You had a three-to-one ratio of assists to turnovers, which is excellent. You guarded the other team's best point guard. You thought 'pass before shot.' You had the humility to sacrifice yourself for the good of the team. We could not have won the national title without you."

I listed all his strengths, then said, "In fact, the only two things preventing you from playing at the next level are that you may be a little slow and you don't have that quick first step, that burst of acceleration. Those are the only two things that are preventing you from being talked about as a future NBA player."

I told him this because I knew that I was dealing with a player who was on the verge of embracing success. He no longer saw any light at the end of the tunnel. He had already won a state championship as a high school player. He had already won a national championship in college. And he didn't think he could play at the next level.

So what was his motive?

He didn't have one. The result is that I would be dealing with a young man who was simply trying to maintain his present level throughout the summer instead of committing himself to great improvement.

"Do you know what I would do if I were you?" I said to him. "If I were you I definitely wouldn't be jealous of my teammates, because you certainly want to see them succeed and make the NBA. But I would also want a piece of that as well.

And if I were you I wouldn't let a lack of foot speed or a lack of a quick burst on my first step prevent me from one day being a pro."

I told him to think of all the good things he does, the ones already listed. All the skills that had helped us win a championship.

"So if I were you," I continued, "the first thing I would do tomorrow would be to go out and begin to do everything that's humanly possible to improve my foot speed and my first step. And I would see this as a golden opportunity. Because you have as much right to make it to the NBA as anyone else on this basketball team, and you can't let that opportunity pass."

Well, he became a motivated player. Why? Because he wanted to give himself every opportunity to open doors in his future. What I did was enable him to dream. If he doesn't make it, the game of "what ifs" will not be a part of his life.

That's what motivators do. They enable people to dream.

Although that window of opportunity may be open only a crack, getting people to believe that it is indeed open is so important. You let them know they have a long way to go. You let them know how difficult it's going to be. But you also let them know that the opportunity is there.

Helping someone build that dream is vital to maintaining their growth and self-confidence.

To do so you have to recognize that everyone has a need for approval and direction. Everyone wants to be recognized. Give people that opportunity. Make them aware that they're going to have to work harder than they ever imagined, but help them build that vision of accomplishment. What you've created is not false, not an unrealistic hope. There's a window there; and the more you work, the wider that window opens.

Once you've created that self-esteem you can start to create that hope. By creating hope you're creating desire. And that's what leads to achieving dreams.

The other thing to understand about raising self-esteem is to realize that everyone has their own agenda, that individual goals and dreams exist among the collective dreams of the larger group. Each individual in an organization is motivated by something different. As a coach, a CEO, a teacher, a parent, a manager, you must know what drives each person. This is imperative to your success as a motivator.

How do you do this?

By research.

If you are a boss you should know as much about the people under you as you can. What do they want? What are their goals? What are they trying to accomplish? Not what *you* want. What *they* want. You know what you want. The key is what they want and how you can help them achieve those goals.

The more you know about what drives them the more you know what buttons to push when it comes to motivating them.

Think back to the Billy Donovan story. Only by finding out more about him was I able to know what tack to take in dealing with him. You have to put the effort in to get to know the people under you as individuals. Any leader can cultivate greatness in his followers if he sticks to this plan, is organized, and has enough data available to know how to motivate each person.

You also must show that you truly care about the people you're leading, that they are not just faceless robots to you, little more than interchangeable parts. And you must do this without condescension, the feeling that you're better than they are. If you come across this way they will instantly tune you out.

I give all my players a psychological test when they come to Kentucky, for the simple reason that I want to know as much about them as possible. I want to know who has low self-esteem and who feels that he can conquer the world. I want to identify their mental strengths and weaknesses so that we can know what to work on.

For instance, when I tested Jamal Mashburn, my first great player at Kentucky, I realized that even though he had great natural ability and was the most talented recruit we had brought into Kentucky at that point, he had very low self-esteem. Knowing that, I was able to deal more effectively with Jamal, boosting him up in front of his teammates, saying over and over that we were no doubt going to be successful because we had the best freshman in the country. Only by finding out this critical part of Jamal's personality was I able to do this.

When dealing with the players and with the many different agendas on the team, my rule of thumb is simple: When it comes to discipline and work ethic, I treat all my players the same; when it comes to their own individual goals I handle them *individually*.

Your job as the motivator is to try to find out what each individual's motive is. Maybe you can't always do that, but the more you know about an individual the better chance you have of helping them be more successful.

As a coach, you can tell a college player to run through a wall and odds are he will ask you how many seconds he has to do it in. With professional players you have to sit them down and tell them why it's important for them to run through that wall, and how much money they can make doing it.

The lesson in that transcends coaching: You can't necessarily motivate everybody the same way. You have to be able to understand who you are dealing with, what's important to them, what they desire.

And remember, this is not army boot camp or the marines. It's not basic training. It's not totally autocratic anymore, the old my-way-or-the-highway approach. That rigid, authoritative style might have worked a generation ago, but now it's as obsolete as old vinyl records. All that approach is going to get you now is low morale and a rebellious spirit, because eventually all you become is a loud radio people want to turn off.

You can't embarrass people in front of their peers, or degrade them, whether you're in a position of leadership, in an organization, or as a parent or in the workplace.

I learned this in the two years I spent as the coach of the New York Knicks from 1987 to 1989. One of the players I worked with was Patrick Ewing, the great Knicks center.

Patrick is a great team player. He's a joy to be around, works hard every day, and is a coach's delight. The antithesis of the common stereotype of the pampered NBA star. But you can't criticize Patrick in front of his peers. He is a very proud person, and he sees that as a wound to his pride. Behind closed doors, one-on-one, you can criticize different aspects of his game, things he should be working on to improve, and he will handle that fine. But not in front of his peers.

Patrick is not unique in this regard. Not in today's culture. We all have our pride, and we usually don't like it when it's punctured in public.

You also have to tell people why they are doing something rather than having them do it simply because you said so. This is the 1990s—the times aren't going to change back to the coaching style of the previous decades. You are going to have to change. If you can't, you will get passed by as surely as if you're trying to sell record players.

For example, if I'm teaching a drill that I know is boring to my players I have to make them aware of the purpose of the drill, make them aware of how it can benefit their game. I can't just expect them to do it with passion because I tell them to. That stubborn dogmatic approach has a very short shelf life with today's players and should be avoided as much as possible.

So how do you create morale as a leader? How do you get people's self-esteem where it needs to be to deserve victory?

Here are five key rules.

▶ Help each person see himself or herself as having a significant role, no matter what it might be. Each person has to understand that he or she is essential to the group's success, that it's the sum of all the parts that make up the whole.

▶ Create a significance for the group, whether it's an organization, a team, or a company. Just being a part of an organization is no longer enough anymore. Each member must feel he or she is a part of something important, and not just putting in time.

▶ Maintain positive reinforcement for the effort people are giving. Always let them know you are aware of it and how much you appreciate it.

▶ Recognize the people who get less attention in the group because they're not in the glamorous positions. The secretaries in the company. The substitutes on a team. Thank them publicly for their unselfishness, and do it in front of their peers. That is their share of the limelight.

▶ Never forget that it's imperative to keep people positive, because those who are discontented have the potential to infect others. And eventually that negativity changes the dynamic of the entire group. There's really truth to the old adage that one bad apple spoils the bunch.

## Key Points for Step 1

Self-esteem is vital to achieving. You must not only feel good about yourself but feel you can perform and can accomplish great things.

Self-esteem is directly linked to deserving success. If you have established a great work ethic and have begun the discipline that is inherent with that, you will automatically begin to feel better about yourself. It's all interrelated. You must deserve victory to feel good about yourself.

You do have control over your life. Your success or failure is up to you.

Having doubts along the way is all part of the game. We all have times when we experience frustrations. The key is to keep sticking to your plan of attack and have the patience to realize that transforming your life is a marathon, not a sprint.

There is no age limit on transforming your life. No rule that says that after a certain age you are simply the way you are and that's it. Change not only is possible at any time but is essential.

△

Self-esteem has to be earned to have significant value.

△

Everyone wants to believe that he or she has value, an important lesson to learn if you are a parent, teacher, boss, or coach.

△

Now that we have established that high self-esteem is essential for achievement—and we realize that self-esteem grows out of our work ethic and our plan of attack—we are ready for the next step. We are ready to start demanding more of ourselves.

# MAKING THE BEST
# OF THE HAND
# YOU'RE DEALT

The first thing you must understand is that the person being motivated must have the feeling that the one doing the motivating really cares about you. That's the way it was between me and Coach Pitino, a relationship that exists to this day.

No matter how hard he drove me when I was a player I always knew that he cared for me as a person, and that what he was doing was going to make me a better player and a better man. That was the main reason I decided to stay at Providence College when Coach Pitino took over as coach in the spring of 1985. The players all knew that he cared about us, and that's why we were willing to go to the extra mile.

A lot of people told me I wasn't good enough to play at a big-time Division I program, that I was a midlevel or even a Division II player. Coach came and said, "Okay, this is the hand we've been dealt, so we'll take it and make it the best it can be."

That's when he started calling me "Billy the Kid," which was a way to boost my self-esteem. It worked. The more I worked the better

I started to feel about myself, and that only made me want to work harder. It all just kind of snowballed.

After my junior year, in which I averaged about fifteen points, I dropped by his office just before going home for the summer. I was feeling pretty good about myself, because as a sophomore I had played very little. What he told me that day has stayed with me ever since. He said, "Billy, don't ever lose sight of what got you to this place."

That was his way of telling me not to stop working hard, to not just go home, relax, and lose the summer.

When I took over at Florida as the head coach I made it a point to handle it the same way Coach handled it when he took over at Providence. A coaching change always brings on a certain amount of uncertainty and anxiety for the players, and I wanted to make the transition as easy for them as possible, while at the same time stressing to them that this is the hand we've been dealt and we're going to make the best of it and not make excuses.

That's just one of the many things Coach has taught me. I hear his voice in my head all the time. And virtually everything I accomplished in basketball, and the methods I'm using in my own coaching career now all come from him.

### Billy Donovan
FORMER PITINO PLAYER AND ASSISTANT COACH;
NOW THE HEAD COACH AT THE UNIVERSITY OF FLORIDA

# STEP 2 SET DEMANDING GOALS

I have found that even the most cynical people have dreams. They might not often admit to them. They might have no idea how to reach them. They might even believe that there is no way they can ever fulfill them.

But we all want to believe that we are special, unique. We all want to believe that we are capable of great feats, of reaching our fullest potential. We need dreams. They give us a vision of a better future. They nourish our spirit; they represent possibility even when we are being dragged down by reality. They keep us going. Most successful people are dreamers, ordinary people who are not afraid to think big and dare to be great. Dreamers are not content with being merely mediocre, because no one ever dreams of going halfway.

When we were little kids in the playground we didn't dream of hitting singles in the first inning. We dreamed of that home run in the bottom of the ninth to win the World Series. We don't dream of a life of struggle and frustration, one in which we underachieve and don't live up to our potential. We dream of doing something big and splashy, something significant. We don't dream in drab shades of gray. We dream in bright colors. We dream big.

As I've already stated, if you are not willing to work hard and establish discipline in your life, then all your dreams are merely going to be pipe dreams, little flights of fancy, nothing more than adolescent fantasies that are never going to come true.

We now know that we have to put in the effort to reach our dreams, but the tough part is that most of us don't know where to start working. We might have every intention of becoming vice president in five years or running across the finish line in a marathon or completing the novel we started years ago. But often we have no idea how to translate these dreams into actions.

In order to make real steps toward fulfilling our ultimate, big, splashy dreams, we have to start with concrete objectives. These are our goals.

## GOALS VERSUS DREAMS

What's the difference?

Dreams are where we want to end up. Goals are how we get there. Dreams are our vision of where we are after our struggle, the prize at the end of the journey. Goals are the individual steps we take to ultimately deserve the prize.

We don't know where our dreams are going to take us; we don't know where the journey is going to end. Our dreams are off in the future someplace, and who knows what's going to happen in the meantime. We may at best accomplish only 50 percent of our dreams. In fact, odds are as we get older and our priorities shift, our dreams probably will change, especially if they're related to our job or career because the business climate is changing so rapidly.

Our dreams are our master plan; they create an ideal to shoot for and represent a new life we want to lead.

Our goals are simply means we are going to use to get there. Goals are our day-by-day blueprint that provide achievable targets for incremental improvement.

But dreams and goals are interrelated.

Let's say I tell one of my players that he must gain weight over the summer. That is his goal; he weighs two hundred pounds, and that's just too light for him as a player. So if I tell him I think he should gain weight and leave it at that, he probably will come back to school in the fall ten pounds heavier. But if his dream is to play professional basketball one day, and I tell him that in order for him to be in a position where that might be possible he's going to have to gain thirty pounds—he will come back weighing two hundred thirty.

If he doesn't make the connection with his dream, he will not meet his goals.

You can have big dreams, but you must understand that your long-term successes are a direct result of what you can achieve every day. We need goals. Goals provide our daily routine. They show us where to start and they establish our priorities. They make us organized and create the discipline in our lives. Getting yourself to establish your goals is paramount, one of the key building blocks in achieving success.

Let's say you're trying to climb the corporate ladder in a large company, and you are not too optimistic about your chances because there seems to be too many people competing for too few jobs at the top. Your dream is that promotion, but wishing isn't going to make it happen. What you have to do is break down the dream into components you can work on individually and then make a list of them. After studying the "dream" position, you determine that what they're looking for is a hardworking, driven person who can manage a team well and improve productivity.

Perfecting each of these characteristics then becomes goals you can shoot for.

The first thing you do is establish a curiosity in your boss. You show your boss that you are eager to work hard and pull greater than your share. One way to do this, obviously, is to come to work early. You also begin to seek out more long-term projects to show you can maintain a certain energy level over a sustained period of time. Then you have to show your boss that you're a team player, that you take the time to pitch in for the group and that you're the kind of person who makes the people around you perform better.

The point is that you must establish specific goals and clearly define them. Goals are not merely fuzzy wishes, or hastily made New Year's resolutions. They are tangible action items to be written down and followed. This list is the road map you pore over before you start out on your trip.

## HOW TO SELECT YOUR GOALS

Goals essentially come in two categories.

There are the goals that we set to focus behavior we want to change, and goals that are established by working backward from where we want to end up in our dreams.

Let's examine the first category.

I've found that most people, when presented with the fact that it's going to take hard work to be successful, will begin working harder. That's not the problem. The most difficult part is getting them to understand their weaknesses so that they can frame their goals around fixing them.

Take Wayne Turner, for example.

He is a sophomore on my basketball team at the University of Kentucky. He was a great high-school star at a prep school outside of Boston, a high-school All-American. He played in a weak league, where he averaged about forty points a game, mostly on taking the ball to the basket, an area of the game in which he is very gifted. Because he was able to do this so easily at the level he played in during high school, he rarely shot the ball from the perimeter—now this is the weakest part of his game.

When Wayne arrived at Kentucky as a freshman he had some serious shooting flaws, but he really didn't see these as a problem because he always had been able to play to his strength. But as the competition got better, his weakness at shooting the perimeter shot became more pronounced. After a year of this fall-off, he realized that he must work at this part of his game if he was ever going to become a great player. But that didn't start to happen until he finally admitted to himself that his game had a weakness.

Many people are unable to admit they have weaknesses. They try to cover them up and deceive both themselves and others. They'll do almost anything to avoid confronting the fact that they have a chink in their armor. I call it the "Ralph Kramden syndrome." You remember Ralph? That great character in *The Honeymooners*, made famous by Jackie Gleason, was a man who always had a scheme, some destined-to-fail, get-rich-quick plan that entailed avoiding any hard work— work that would have eventually gotten him there if he had bothered to lift a finger. Ralph was always deluded into thinking there was a shortcut to success.

After you take an honest look at your weaknesses, as you did in Step 1, you face the second hurdle: doing something about them.

You can quickly spot people who don't want to really confront their weaknesses. They're the excuse makers. The procrastinators. They're always putting off things until tomorrow. We all do this to one degree or another, but these are serious problems we have to confront. If we don't conquer these weaknesses one by one, they will consume our time and energy and make us miss opportunities. We cannot let these traits fester. Postponing action is only postponing achievement.

Therefore, we need goals that are going to help us overcome our weaknesses. If it's something straightforward, like Wayne Turner's shooting a basketball, the goal becomes relatively simple: Establish a plan of attack that relies on working on proper technique with hours of repetition.

If the problem is more intangible—procrastination, poor organization, avoiding personal responsibilities, and so on—you need to define goals that are clearly designed to change that specific behavior.

For instance, if you have a tendency to procrastinate, create a goal for yourself to write down three things you are going to accomplish today, three things that you normally would put off. These will be three things that you will definitely do before you go to sleep that night. What these three things are is irrelevant. Your list might include calling to check up on a client who constantly complains or taking a walk around the block instead of drinking another cup of coffee in the morning. You're simply trying to change behavior.

By challenging yourself to complete things you would rather not, you are telling yourself not only that you recognize weakness but also that you have a plan to do something about it. That plan is simply a checklist of goals you establish for yourself.

The key is to make these goals easily attainable. We're not looking for a life transformation in twenty-four hours. We're not looking for a total change in behavior overnight. What we are looking for are *daily* successes. Remember, our long-term success is the result of the small victories we accumulate every day. Once you achieve that goal of doing three things each day that you normally would have put off doing, then increase the goal: Make it five things every day, then make it seven. Soon you will have eliminated that weakness altogether.

The second category of goals—ones based on the pursuit of your specific dreams—is a little different.

First, write down step by step what it's going to take to reach your dream, whatever that dream may be. Break it down to as many components as possible.

For instance, when I retire from coaching I want to have a second career in broadcasting. I don't have any delusions about being the next Bob Costas or John Madden, but I've enjoyed the little broadcasting I've done and now know that one day I'm going to explore it further. I will probably be about fifty then, far too young to spend my time sitting in Heaven's Waiting Room. So instead of playing a couple of rounds of golf every day, I will actively pursue a broadcasting career the same way I pursued a coaching career when I graduated from the University of Massachusetts in 1974.

How am I going to do it?

By being organized. By establishing short-term goals.

I will create my organized plan of attack. I will read everything I can on the subject. I will establish the work ethic that is required for this specific job. I will create an aura of excitement about what I am pursuing, the feeling I am embarking on some great new adventure in my life that will be completely different from any of my previous jobs. I will have patience, too, the awareness that this is a journey I'll be on for a long time, without a rigid timetable or deadline. And I will have no doubt that I will ultimately reach my goal.

It won't happen all at once. I'll take it step by step, knowing that the secret to realizing any long-term ambition is achieving dozens of short-term goals.

## DON'T MAKE UNREALISTIC GOALS

Let's say you are one hundred pounds overweight and your goal is to lose that weight.

Well, you're not going to lose half of that in two months.

Just as that underachieving adolescent lying on the couch with no discipline is not going to make the honor roll by the end of the semester. To set such lofty goals only leads to frustration and then the inevitable failure. These goals are unrealistic, at least for the short term, and are also counterproductive. If you are climbing a ladder you can't be expected to go from the first step to the tenth step in one burst. You are looking for a gradual progression through all the steps, along with the realization that each step leads to another and then to another; and though each step might be small, a succession of them takes you much closer to your goal. You must constantly be aware of this, constantly be aware that you are making progress, even if the process is slower than you might have hoped for.

We also must remember that we're not always going to reach our goals all of a sudden. We're looking to change behavior; instant gratification is not what we're after.

So we must have patience and understand that we are trying to establish lifelong patterns, new behaviors that are going to allow us to become more successful. We must have confidence that because our work ethic has been established, our plan of attack is a good one, and we know that failure is just a way to get better, and that ultimately we will be successful.

Sometimes the goals we set for ourselves might be too high for us to reach. We may have to alter them a bit. We may even have to one day change them. But even those goals that we don't meet can lead to great satisfaction.

How?

Because of the effort we put forth. Because of the striving to improve ourselves. This, in itself, will take us to another level. So you must constantly praise yourself when you get to the next step. You are making progress, and you should be rewarded. Even the achievement of the smallest goals is something to be proud of.

Achievement of any kind means you are working.

And it ought to be clear by now that hard work is a key element to success.

Striving toward short-term goals, then, is inherently a strength-building exercise.

Let's consider the stereotypical floundering teenage boy, the kind of child everyone seems to have a problem with—parents, teachers, coaches, everyone. You know the type: poor grades, earrings or noserings, dyed hair. The 1990s couch potato, who seems to have no definable interests other than watching television, playing video games, and hanging out with his friends. The classic underachiever.

What he has to do is change his pattern of behavior, to install discipline where there is probably very little. This child—like the rest of us—flounders because he is poorly organized and has little or no discipline in his life. His goals are not defined. And this isn't a lapse that happens overnight. This kid's problems probably didn't start last week. There has probably been an absence of discipline for a long time.

In these circumstances, a parent has to create some

short-term goals that are easily attainable. Understand that this child is a product of a culture that genuflects at the altar of instant gratification. Everything has to happen right away, which is why fast food, the TV clicker, and the lottery ticket are so popular. This kind of child has never learned the virtue of patience or discipline in his life; he probably has no clue to what these things are even about. You must understand this and act accordingly.

So where do you begin?

You help him set short-term goals that are attainable. Twelve-hour goals. Twenty-four-hour goals. Forty-eight-hour goals. Goals that make it possible for this child to experience success. If the goals are too long-term or too difficult, you are merely drawing up a blueprint for failure. And don't look for immediate and dramatic change. Look for incremental progress, change that comes not by the yard but by the inch. With time and patience and discipline the inches add up. A genuine work ethic begins to emerge.

What I do in that situation is tell that young person to go home, sleep, and dream. Think a few thoughts about the future, then come back tomorrow and tell me what you see as your future. Then I say, "If that's your dream, then let's work together to make it come true."

It might be something very simple, like making better grades in school. "Okay," I say, "take your weakest class, the one you made a C in, and see if you can raise it to a B. That's your goal. To rise above average in that class."

After you give them their goals, have them write down the methods they will use to implement those goals. Then make sure those methods are being followed. After it's over, after the goal has been reached, do something special to show your appreciation and respect for what that person accomplished.

Take them to dinner, have a party, anything that will serve as the reward, the payoff for their hard work and dedication.

Remember the three basic rules: establish goals, make the person show you how the methods will be implemented, then follow up. Make sure the person understands that it can't be a wish list. It has to be a work list.

And what works for rebellious teenage boys works for anyone—even you. You may not have poor grades, a variety of earrings or noserings, or punk-style hair, but we all have a certain lack of discipline about work, exercise, or whatever. But setting short-term attainable goals and then achieving them fuels the desire for more achievement. In fact, it inspires us to want to achieve more.

Small successes breed larger successes. Attainable short-term goals will eventually lead to establishing longer-term goals. Keep achieving short-term goals, and soon you'll be miles ahead of where you began.

## DON'T SET THE BAR TOO LOW

Although we don't want to set unrealistic goals that frustrate us, we also have to keep pushing ourselves.

This is the key. We always can do more than we think we can do. Anyone who has ever achieved anything significant knows this. We always can work harder. We always can put in longer hours, expend more energy. We always can perform better. Why is this? Because we only know what we already have been able to do. We can't see into the future, meaning we don't have a realistic image of ourselves meeting some of our tougher goals.

The trick is to keep demanding the effort from ourselves, to not be content with small victories, to not settle for mediocrity. We are trying to be the best we can possibly be, to get the most out of our potential. We are not reaching for some comfort zone where we can coast easily.

I often bring my players into my office, sit them down across from me, and ask them what their goals are. I want them to *tell* me what they are. To have to define them. To have to verbalize them.

And often they sell themselves short. They set their goals too low.

Let's go back to Billy Donovan. You remember him? He was the player on my Providence College team who went from a little-used reserve to an All-Big East player in two years, primarily due to his work ethic and vastly improved sense of self-esteem.

Now if I had asked him what his goals were in our first meeting he would have undoubtedly said, "To be a better college basketball player. To maybe play half the game, average maybe ten points." Why not? We're talking about someone who rarely had played at all in his first two seasons. Thus the idea of playing half the game and having some success no doubt sounded very appealing to him at the time. The point is, he never would have said, "I want to be an All Big East player and have a chance to play in the NBA." That would have been a dream, not a goal.

But when we first talked, he didn't have a dream, at least one he could articulate. He had only a goal, and a not very demanding one at that.

Very often people will sell themselves short, especially people with low self-esteem. Ask them to define their goals, and they will list ones they feel they can easily meet. They set the bar at a height they either can reach very easily or can reach without having to put in a lot of effort. So they immediately reach their goal. The price they pay for this, however, is they can do this without having to be creative, without having to make the great effort.

The result?

This leads to fool's gold—the feeling of accomplishment when you really haven't deserved it.

Some of this is necessary. Remember what we discussed in Step 1: Low self-esteem requires easy, attainable goals to build yourself back up. And floundering, listless people need those short-term goals to get them started. The key is getting yourself and others to participate, to get in the game. But as a person's self-esteem is raised, the expectations also can be raised.

Motivated people raise the bar to supposedly unreachable heights and then establish the methods necessary to reach those heights. They purposely set difficult goals for themselves, because they realize that if the challenge isn't worthy, the payoff will be empty and unsatisfactory. Hollow victories are worse than meaningless. They can be deadly because they allow us to embrace what we have without fully understanding what competition is really all about And before you can say "cheers," an unexpected, difficult challenge comes along and knocks you on your back.

For instance, you might be a salesperson who consistently performs better than the rest of your department using the same tried-and-true methods you used last year. This year you again set out to come in 10 percent better than you did the year before, knowing it will be a breeze. What you don't pay attention to is that all the other salespeople are fed up with coming in second or third or tenth every year. They put everything they can into their jobs this year, improve 20, 30, even 40 percent and leave you behind in the dust.

So you always have to be pushing yourself. Not in unrealistic ways that inevitably lead to failure. But in attainable goals that lead to more demanding goals. All the way up the ladder until you reach where you want to go. One rung at a time.

## HARD WORK ISN'T FUN

We all have a point at which we want to quit. We all have a breaking point. We all have a time when we question what we're doing, especially if it's difficult. Usually the number one sign is when we say, "This is no longer fun. It's just not worth it."

This is human nature, an inevitable part of the process. Especially in a culture that holds out pleasure and fun as the two most desired goals. Most of us have been conditioned to think that everything is supposed to be a good time. Everything is supposed to be "meaningful." If it's not, we're inclined to start questioning its value.

You must understand this and realize that at some point it's going to happen to you. You must understand the power of these psychological traps and do everything you can to combat them. You must keep telling yourself that all the pain you're going through is worth it and that if you keep to your plan of attack, there is going to be a great payoff at the end. But this will come only if you stay the course and keep to your plan. You must keep telling yourself this is not always going to be fun; but what you are looking for is to reach your dreams, and this is the price you must pay.

Again, it goes back to what we talked about in Step 1, the initial premise of this book: You must deserve victory. It is not always going to be fun. It is not always going to happen for you overnight. It is exactly that attitude that probably prevented you from reaching your dreams in the first place, this sense that if something isn't always fun and pleasurable it's simply not worth it.

As a coach I'm always trying to explain to my players that all the pain they're going through is worth it. That there's a great reward for them if they keep at it. I must keep explaining to them how special the payoff is going to be for them at the end. Only then are they going to able to get through those moments when they hit the wall and want to quit.

Consider the case of Richie Farmer.

Richie played for me at Kentucky, graduating in 1992, but he already was a legend in the state by the time he arrived in Lexington as a freshman. He grew up in the mountains of eastern Kentucky, in Clay County, right in the middle of Hat-field-McCoy country, where there were only twelve boys in his graduating class from grade school. If you're not kin or a member of the University of Kentucky basketball team, you'd better be careful. He once told me that you always knew where you stood with the people from his hometown. If they liked you they would give you the shirt off their back. If they didn't, they would kill you.

Well, Richie was Most Valuable Player of the state high school tournament two years in a row, the state's Mr. Basketball, which in Kentucky is about as big as it gets. He also led Clay County to its only state title ever; coincidentally, it was the same year the movie *Hoosiers* came out, the film with Gene Hackman about the little Indiana team. And there were similarities: Richie's team was all-white as well and didn't have a player over six foot two. So this was a big deal, and when he announced that he was going to come to UK, it was in his high-school gym in front of sixteen hundred people, who gave him a standing ovation.

The point is that Richie Farmer was a folk hero in the state, so when my wife, Joanne, called me one day to say that

Richie and his father were sitting in my downstairs room and that Richie wanted to quit, I came home in a hurry. Seems Richie had had a run-in with our strength coach in the pre-season workouts, and he wanted to quit. He also was trying to come to grips with the realization he was not going to be the kind of superstar in college that he had been in high school, that he now was going to be a complementary player—what we in basketball call a "role player"—never an easy thing to deal with for someone who had been as lionized in high school as Richie had been.

"It's no longer fun," he said.

"Let's see," I said to him, "You're fifteen pounds over-weight, you're in terrible shape, and now you're being asked to lift weights and push your body, and you're telling me it's not fun. Of course it's not fun. How could it be fun? It's not supposed to be fun. The fun is supposed to be when you run out on the court in Rupp Arena in front of the greatest fans in the world. When you're in great shape and you're ready to play, that's when it's fun. This is what you have to go through to get to that fun. So when you tell me you don't like it—you're not supposed to like it. Because there's no reason to like it.

"In fact, I just came off the road from recruiting. Eighteen days of airplanes and hotel rooms and rental cars and being away from my family. It's the part of the job I don't like. It's the price I have to pay for putting a great team out on the floor in Rupp Arena. But I don't like it.

"So you know what, Richie? Let's quit together. We'll have a joint press conference, and we'll both announce we're quitting. The Italian coach from New York and the Kentucky kid from the mountains. Both of us together. It will be an amazing press conference."

At which point Richie started to laugh.

"Coach, you can't quit," he said.

"I know," I said. "And neither can you."

In forty-five minutes he had cried, he had laughed, and in the end he felt relieved.

I didn't denigrate him. I didn't antagonize him by calling him a sissy or a wimp for wanting to quit. I never said he had to shape up or ship out. If I had done those things he undoubtedly would have gotten angry and quit, and I would have lost him forever. Nor did I say that his perceptions of things were wrong. Just the opposite.

Richie came to understand that lifting weights and pushing his body to its limits when he wasn't in shape was not fun. That having his insides tearing at him and feeling he was going to be sick was not fun. But at that point he realized he couldn't lessen his work load because that would have meant postponing the dream of being a part of a great team in Rupp Arena.

Working hard is not always fun. That's why it's called "work."

For Richie Farmer it was a chance to be a significant part of a team that had gone from being featured in *Sports Illustrated* in May 1989 with the headline "Kentucky's Shame," to a team that was one point away from going to the Final Four in 1992. Hard work enabled Richie Farmer to see his career end with his number being raised to the top of Rupp Arena for his contribution to that turnaround, the assurance that he forever will be a part of the University of Kentucky basketball history.

But it's not always fun, and that's why it's important to tell people that there will be rewards at the end of the tunnel. With a group, that should be easier to accomplish, and we hope that the newer members can learn from the older ones.

But not all of us have a team network to keep us going.

Take the salespeople on the road, for example, the ones

whose only life is selling, where it's just them and the customers and the product in the middle.

Those people doesn't have that built-in support system.

So how can they convince themselves that their work is leading to something greater?

Those people must form a bond with the product they are selling. They must develop the belief that the product is the best on the marketplace. They must feel not only that the sale is something that needs to happen but also that the person on the other end is gaining something worthwhile. These are the components of a salesperson's goal to become the best salesperson in his or her field. The phone calls, office visits, and research are simply the means to get to where he or she wants to be.

It's the same process for you.

You must keep reminding yourself that your desire to be more successful is a worthy goal—and one that you deserve once you've established your ethic—and that you have faith in your organized plan of attack. That becoming more successful is a process, one that usually takes place in small incremental steps and usually involves some times when it's not going to be fun.

Let's not kid ourselves. Transforming yourself takes hard work and effort. If it were easy, there would be a pill for it. Or else someone would franchise it, and there would be a Success Store on every corner.

Just like Richie Farmer had to go through all the weight lifting and running to get in better shape, you must pay a price too. It may not be physical exertion, but it will be a price all the same. To think anything else is self-delusion. You must understand you're going to have to endure many boring day-to-day tasks that you are not going to like all the time.

So you must keep your eye on the prize. You must keep

telling yourself that the end is going to be worth the means. We see this in sports all the time, the amazing outpouring of emotion after a team wins a championship. Part of that is the thrill of the victory, obviously. But it's more than that too. It's the realization of how hard they worked to get there, all the long hours, all the hard work, all the sweat. That's what you think about when you win a championship: how hard you have worked for it.

That's an important lesson.

Remember the movie *Rocky*? The core of the movie is the incredible quest Rocky goes on and finding out how far he will go in the search of his dream. All those early-morning runs through the city of Philadelphia. All those sit-ups. All those hours punching the meat in the food warehouse. That's what got us so emotionally hooked on the movie and made the character so much a part of the culture: the fact that Rocky would do what it took to transform his life and reach his dream, no matter how arduous, no matter how painful. That sense that the dream was worth all the hard work to him.

And all the while he was putting himself through such a grueling preparation, Rocky was able to keep his eye on his dream.

That's what you must constantly do too: Keep your eye on the prize.

You often hear a lot about mental toughness in sports. Well, mental toughness has nothing to do with how far you can run or how much weight you can lift or any other display of physical strength. Being mentally tough is doing the workouts on those days when you don't feel like doing them. It's making that extra call when it's five o'clock and everyone else around you is going home. It's doing that extra work over the weekend even though it's supposed to be a day off. It's getting out of bed early and starting the day on those mornings when you'd rather pull the covers back over your head for another hour or so. It's demanding that your children stick to their discipline when it's easier just to let them watch television and not have to hassle them about it. It's doing all those mundane repetitious tasks that you know have to be done that day, although you'd rather postpone them until tomorrow.

It's fighting through all those times when it's not fun. It's understanding that there always are going to be times when you have to persevere, but knowing your toughness will get you to your dreams.

## KEEP YOUR VISION

You must have a vision of a better future.

It's not enough to just work hard. It's not enough to simply say you've established some goals and also have the discipline to meet those goals. You must realize that if you can change your behavior you ultimately can reach your dreams.

In groups, this is done by constantly telling people that what they're involved in is extremely worthwhile, whether it's to be the best company, the best team, whatever. In individuals, it's constantly telling them that their hard work is going to be worth it, that it's going to benefit them. That's what gets them through the hard times.

But how do you create your own vision? What can you do to get yourself through those hard times?

You must be more organized. You must create your own yardstick and rules for action.

One way to do this is set up a game in which you must compete against yourself. It's a little like playing Nintendo. You play by yourself but are working within the confines of a machine. You begin to understand that machine, its glitches, its tendencies. In the same way, you must play a game each day in which you compete against your previous day's record, taking into account stumbling blocks, working around them, and trying to better yourself every time.

For instance, look at the saleswoman on the road who makes ten calls a day, hoping to get four positive bites. But on this particular day she only gets two. So now she must tell herself that her goal for tomorrow is six positive bites, her normal four plus the two she didn't get the day before.

This is not easy.

The key is to keep up your discipline. To keep creating daily goals and, once you've accomplished them, to build on them to then create midterm goals and ultimately long-term goals.

## Key Points for Step 2

Goals are simply the means you use to reach your dreams. You start out with short-term goals that are easily attainable to get into the habit of improvement; then you make the goals more demanding as you begin to have success.

△

Be able to admit your weaknesses and establish short-term goals to overcome them. Don't make your goals unrealistic; keep raising the bar to make sure you're pushing yourself. You always can do more than you think you can do. Don't be content with just small successes. Use those small successes to generate larger successes. The key is to keep creating demanding goals for yourself, goals that will allow you to reach your full potential.

△

Hard work is not always fun, but it's the price you must pay to be more successful.

So you constantly must keep your eye on your dream and must constantly be telling yourself that your hard work and effort is one day going to be worth it, that there's going to be a big payoff at the end. This is essential because there are going to be times when you question what you are doing, when you ask yourself, "What's this for?"

△

When that question arises, envision yourself enjoying the reward at the end. This will make your journey worth it.

# EVERY GOAL HAS
# A PURPOSE

From the first minute, he started changing everyone's attitude.

I was a junior at the time at Boston University. We had been seven and nineteen and ten and fifteen in the two years before Coach Pitino arrived. We didn't know how to win. I remember we had a team meeting, and he told us, "If you do it my way you're going to win. We're going to be the hardest working team in the country."

We didn't know what to think.

Then he met with everyone individually, and told us what he both liked and didn't like from what he had seen or film. He told me that I wouldn't play a minute, ever, if I didn't (1) gain twenty pounds over the summer, (2) become quicker, and (3) learn how to score. I was almost in shock. I had started at point guard for two years, and thought I had done all right. And here was this new coach telling me that if I didn't gain twenty pounds not to bother coming out for the team next year.

I came from New York and basketball was the most important thing in my life. I suppose, too, I was looking for someone to be a savior. So all that summer I lifted weights and worked out and went from 160 to 178. I felt great, because at the beginning of the summer I didn't think I could do it. But he told me he had said twenty pounds, not eighteen. So every morning I had to get up at six in the morning and run two miles, a week of running for every pound I hadn't gained. You'd think if I was two pounds short he would have made me get up every morning and eat French toast or something, but what it did right away was develop mental toughness. All of us had certain goals we were supposed to reach, and he held you accountable if you didn't reach them.

Then we had this thing called "minute on the brick drill." Every practice was monitored by the managers. If you didn't take a charge or made a stupid mistake or didn't go after a rebound hard enough, you were given a minute. At the end of practice you went into the lane in a defensive stance with a brick in each hand. Well, not really holding them. Balancing them on the top of your palms, which is hard, believe me. Then you had to go from one side of the paint to the other in a defensive stance. Had to do it something like eighteen or twenty times in one minute. And if you stood up, or dropped the bricks, you had to start all over. It was a killer. Your legs were humming.

But you know what?

It worked. Everyone hated the minute on the brick drill so much that if you had a chance to take a charge in practice, you stepped in and took it. If you were coming down on a break out of control, instead of throwing a lousy pass, you stopped and pulled the ball back. We were all so fearful of picking up minutes and having to deal with those bricks we played better.

One game, the next year, he chewed me out at the half, big time, said I was playing selfishly. I went back and played the entire second half, and though I didn't think we were playing particularly well, I was happy we won. But in the locker room he came up to me.

"Get your sweatpants on," he said.

"Why?"

"Because you're going out on the track and run two miles," he said.

Now, this was January and it was cold. But I went out and ran, and he had a manager time me. And not just around the track. Sprints and everything. So the next day in practice I'm still mad, but he calls me over, and it's like nothing ever happened. Because the bottom line was that the love was there. We knew that he really cared about us. He wanted us to get better.

But I see now that everything was for a purpose. The drills with the bricks helped your defensive stance. Even making me run those two miles that night. He instilled in us that for us to be successful we had to do that. And he was right. When we practiced poorly, we played poorly.

None of us were big names. We just came out of nowhere. But in games we would put the press on, and you could just see the look in the other teams' faces in the last five minutes. t was the look of a guy in a fight who knew he was ready to get knocked out.

And you know, I have a very special feeling for all the people I played with at Boston University. We all worked so hard. There were times you thought he was crazy. There were times when you didn't want to do it anymore.

But I left BU knowing I became the best player I could have been, and isn't that really what every college player wants? Unlike a lot of guys who played in college and spent the rest of their lives saying I could have been better if the coach had let me shoot more or let me play more, I am a happy guy, a fulfilled player. The bottom line is I had a tremendous college basketball experience, and it was all because of Rick Pitino.

Glenn Consor
EX-PITINO PLAYER

# STEP 3 ALWAYS BE POSITIVE

N orman Vincent Peale thought that being positive could cure cancer.

His book was called *The Power of Positive Thinking,* and its primary theme was that individuals should never allow obstacles or hardships to dominate their lives.

He believed that people had to have faith in their abilities and be self-confident. He believed that any feelings of inferiority had to be overcome and that if you think "defeat" you are bound to be defeated. He also believed that people must fill their minds with creative and healthy thoughts and that each day should be started by affirming peaceful, happy, and contented attitudes.

His entire approach is based on the idea that for every problem there is a solution and that these solutions lie within ourselves, both in our faith and our belief in ourselves.

Now I do not know that being positive can cure cancer.

But I do know that being positive is essential to success.

How did I learn this?

By making mistakes as a young coach.

This is the way I used to coach at Boston University in my first head-coaching job: Let's say it is a close game, only about ten seconds remaining and we're down one. We are in a time-out setting up a play for that one shot that we have to make if we're going to win. My team is all around me; the atmosphere is tense. Listen in:

"Okay, this is what we're going to do. Listen up now. *Pay attention.* Because we have to win this game. And if we don't you're not going to believe how hard practice is going to be tomorrow. You're just not going to believe it. So come on. We really need this game. Okay, this is what we're going to do. *Now pay attention.* I'm not going to say it again. *Everyone pay attention.* Joey is going to take the ball out. Steve is going to set the screen. Jamal is going to come off the screen and get the pass from Tony and take the shot. *Now everyone got this? We can't have any mistakes here.* Not like last week. Now, Jamal, the shot will be there, so don't miss it. You missed the one last week because you short-armed it. Now follow through this time and don't miss. Make the damn shot, okay? Because we really, really need this one. You all know how much we need this win tonight. Okay, everyone know what to do? Okay, let's go. And remember? We got to win this one. I mean we *really* got to win this one."

So we break the huddle, and they all start to walk back on the court with their shoulders slumped, as though they were walking off to jail.

And this is what's going on as the players walk back to the court. Joey—the guy who is taking the ball out of bounds—is saying to himself, "Thank God, all I have to do is take the ball of bounds. Last game he had me taking the shot and then stared at me when I missed it like the whole game was my fault." Steve—the guy who is going to set the screen—is saying to himself, "Thank God, all I have to is set the screen. Last game he had me making the pass and then ran the film back over and over afterward to let everyone see it was a lousy pass just to humiliate me." Jamal—the guy who is taking the shot—is saying, "Why me? Why did he pick me? Everyone knows Tony's better in these situations. Why didn't he pick him? Everyone knows I missed the shot last week and now he picks me to take it again. Why me?"

Well, you can guess what used to happen. We would miss the shot, lose the game, and then we would all blame each other.

Because my entire approach in those time-outs was negative.

I was preparing my players to fail.

Everything from stressing that we *had* to win the game, to telling them that if they didn't win all hell was going to break lose. All I had told them about was the pitfalls.

Is it any wonder we lost a lot of close games back then?

But now I'm totally different.

I focus on being positive, making the players feel we are going to win because we know what we're going to do in those situations. We have practiced the plays over and over, and we have every confidence that we are going to be successful in executing them.

And we have been.

Look at our national championship game against Syracuse as an example.

We were ahead in the second half, but we never could really put Syracuse away and take control of the game. With about eight minutes left to play you could sense that the momentum was starting to change, that Syracuse was gaining more confidence the longer they stayed close, and we were starting to lose some of ours. We were also falling into the tendency teams have when they're ahead in close games—to start playing conservatively, to start looking at the clock and hope time goes by more quickly, hoping that the clock is going to win the game for you.

So in our last three time-outs the only thing I stressed—and I did it over and over again—was that we had to cherish the moment. Cherish the fact that we were playing for the national championship. Cherish the fact we were playing on national television. Cherish the fact we were playing on the biggest stage in college basketball.

That, and the fact that we had to keep scoring. Had to keep being aggressive. Had to keep playing as if we wanted that game to last forever.

I told them that if we started being conscious of the clock and relying on it to run out on Syracuse, then Syracuse was going to win the game. But if we kept trying to score and kept playing as if we never wanted the game to end, then we would win and we would be national champions.

There are a lot of factors that tempt us to be negative. It could be a parent, a teacher, a friend, someone close to you growing up. Any of these people could influence your looking at the down side of life. We also live in a cynical culture, with everything from newspapers and talk radio to TV shows and music videos living off controversy. You know the attitude. "What's the use? All politicians are corrupt, the system doesn't work, the deck is stacked against us." We've all heard it. In fact, it's impossible not to hear it.

And it's very easy to fall into this type of outlook and use it as an excuse to fail.

It's what we talked about in the first chapter: People with low self-esteem always blame someone else for their failures. It's never their fault. It's either someone else, or the system, or the boss doesn't understand them, something. Something other than themselves. Our cynical culture gives us plenty of ammunition.

Athletes are always talking about that "positive zone," that state where they are focused, in their comfort zone, with their self-esteem sky high. For a baseball player it's when the ball looks as big as a grapefruit. For a basketball player the basket looks as big as the ocean. For a tennis player it's when the ball seems to lie out there as if it were on some platter. This is the state athletes are in when they have their optimum performance, and often it's an elusive moment, one that can come and go with no warning. But when an athlete is in this so-called zone great things happen.

We have to find a way to get into that positive zone more often.

## BEING POSITIVE IS A DISCIPLINE

Have you ever told someone that you just woke up on the wrong side of the bed?

We often can't help feeling crabby, but mood swings can be reversed. We can control our moods.

Think about that for a second.

There are so many things we can't control, forces we are powerless to change because so much of life is unpredictable. We can't control disease. We can't control injuries. We can't control the weather. We can't control the world economy and the national debt and so many things that are a part of our lives.

*But we can control our moods*. A mood is simply a reflection of our attitude and we can certainly change our attitude. Anthony Epps, one of my Kentucky players who I mentioned earlier, has a tendency to be moody. I'm forever asking him,

"Do you really want to spend so much of your time being miserable? For what? Why would you want to do this?" And he has become better at this, simply by being cognizant of it.

How do we try to control our moods?

The strategy is really no different from the one we use in trying to lose weight or get a promotion or accomplish any other goal. We devise a discipline—an organized plan of attack—and work toward that goal. In this case, it's the development of "positive" as an attitude. This is something we can teach ourselves to do.

For example, when someone asks you at work how you're doing, why not answer, "I feel great."

Do you always feel great?

No.

But why make your co-worker feel bad or uncomfortable too? All this does is bring more people down and then, with one comment, you've begun a whole cycle of negativity.

Again, it's an attitude. A good attitude and a bad attitude are really just two different ways of looking at the same situation.

One of the things I often do in my speeches to companies to illustrate this theme is to split the audience into two groups.

One half of the group becomes Louisville fans, the other half are Kentucky fans.

Now, Louisville is our rival and in this exercise, they become the epitome of negative people. Let's say the speech is in Boston, at the Westin Hotel, to a group of Honda people. So here is a Louisville fan, after being at the Honda conference all day long, talking to his wife late at night in the hotel bar.

"I can't believe how tired I am. What a long day. All those speeches. I thought they would never end. And why are we in Boston? I hate Boston. It's too crowded. And all these old buildings. I heard the Toyota people are going to the Caribbean. And here we are stuck in Boston. I told you I should have gone to work for them. I mean, this is awful."

Now here is the Kentucky fan in the same situation, in the hotel bar late at night with his wife.

"What a great conference. I can't believe what a good time this is. And those speeches. I learned so much, and I know when I get back to work I'm going to be better equipped to do my job. And what a great city. All the history. What a great place to have a conference. Can you believe those Toyota people have to go all the way to the Caribbean? Thank God, I don't. You know how I burn in the sun. And what a great hotel."

These are two different approaches to the same situation. Two ways of looking at the same thing.

Let's look at another example, a very simple one.

You have a big work project due on the boss's desk tomorrow morning. You are up against a formidable deadline, the work equivalent of having a gun pointed at your head. And you are half-done. Now there are two ways to look at the project. You can either bemoan your fate and worry about all the work you still have left to do. Or you can tell yourself that half of it is already done, and you certainly are better off than when you first started the project.

That's your choice: Is the glass half-empty or half-full?

That's the choice we have every morning when we get out of bed.

It's really very simple: We can get out of bed on the positive side and bring that kind of attitude to our day. Or we can get out on the negative side and join what I call the "Fellowship of the Miserable," the kind of people no one wants to be around because they have such lousy attitudes. It's our choice.

Now don't misunderstand.

I'm not saying we should all be Pollyanna every day and walk around with our head in the clouds, devoid of all reality. That's not only unrealistic but probably foolish as well.

But looking honestly at the reality of the situation and seeing the positive in it enhances our quality of life. Self-motivated people look at each day as a new opportunity. Unmotivated people are the ones looking at their watches, wishing the clock would speed up, waiting for the day to be over. They just want the day to end.

Unmotivated people generally see a huge division between their work and their play, their vocation and their avocation. Self-motivated people see little difference. They love what they do. They can't wait to get to work in the morning. They can't wait to get started. They're the ones who believe there aren't enough hours in the day to achieve the goals they're trying to reach.

I never look at my watch during the day because I am so involved in what I'm doing and so immersed in it. To keep yourself on the path to success, you must do this too where you work, and to do this you must bring an aura of excitement to the job.

You can program yourself to do this, just as you can condition yourself to look at things differently, whether it's change or even minor setbacks we face all the time. *You can program yourself to be positive*. This is no different than establishing an exercise routine or a weight loss program or anything else in our lives that we are trying to improve. *Being positive is a discipline*. And we attack it the way we attack any other goal we're trying to reach. With a plan. With the right techniques. With great effort.

And if you do this over a period of time—make a concerted effort to look at things in a more positive, upbeat manner—you will begin to see people's attitudes about you change. Because everyone likes being around positive, upbeat people. They feel lifted by them and they feed off their energy. If you're positive about life and work, people will want you on their team; they'll want to work with you on projects; they'll want to include you when they're taking a client out to dinner to impress them.

I have seen this with every team I've ever coached. I have gone into situations when the players' collective esteem was low, and doubts were everywhere. These are classic situations where negativity rules. But if individual players start to spread positive vibes, the whole team will build that sense of self-esteem, and the attitude will change dramatically.

The increased self-esteem leads to a different attitude that leads to increased performance. With that increased performance comes a more positive attitude, a team that feels as if good things are going to happen. And you know what? Good things start to happen to it. With that comes a better working environment for everyone.

So why not do your part to create a more positive attitude in your workplace? You have to be there anyway. Why not make it as enjoyable as you can? A positive workplace makes everyone feel better and creates a more productive environment.

I tell my players this all the time, especially on those days when I know we're going to have a difficult practice. Like those times when we're not playing for a few days or it's late in the season and the thought of looking at the same people every day is starting to get very tiresome.

My question to them is simple: We're going to be here for two hours so why not make it the best two hours it can be? Because what's the alternative? Make it a bad two hours? Our practice is going to directly reflect the attitude we bring to it.

If we bring a negative attitude to it, see it as nothing more than two hours of hard labor, that is what it will no doubt become.

This is another lesson I learned as a young coach. In those early years at Boston University I was so concerned about having my players have a great work ethic that I never thought about trying to make it more fun for them. Eventually, the players would start to say "this isn't fun" and I would counter that "it's not supposed to be fun. It's work."

But you know what's wrong with that argument?

Eventually, people get ground down by that. When something is entertaining it becomes your passion. When something is merely drudgery it becomes your prison.

I learned that *negative people create negative feelings* and that, as the coach, I had to build on positives, not negatives. Before you can start to develop skills and get people to feel good about themselves you must make them believe they can perform. If you keep telling a basketball player he's a bad three-point shooter he'll never become a good one. If you keep telling your child she's stupid, she probably will be. If you keep telling your salesman he's lousy and you don't know how he's ever going to sell anything, odds are he won't.

But by being positive, we are helping people create a vision of themselves that is better, and they will begin to work toward that. We have to do this to ourselves as well. Instead of beating up on our faults, we have to be fair to our good points and focus on these strengths.

We all need to feel that we *can* accomplish things; that if we are willing to put forth the effort and have the right plan of attack, we *can* prepare ourselves to face the tougher challenges we set up for ourselves en route to our dreams.

*And the more adversity you face, the more positive you have to be.*

As we said in the first step about building self-esteem, if you're coaching a team and you are losing and you try to be tough, you are just asking for dissension. When you are winning you can ride them harder because their confidence is high, they feel good about themselves. Conversely, when you are losing you have to be more supportive and pump them up more.

There's a lesson there for you: Positive people can take on the world.

## CUT LOOSE DISRUPTIVE PEOPLE

We all know the person who comes to work every day and is always griping about something. The conference room is either too hot or too drafty. The coffee's cold. My boss doesn't listen to me. Nothing is ever right. You know the type.

You are always going to be surrounded by negative people. They're in your workplace. They're in your family. They're among your circle of friends. There is no way we can get rid of them.

They're the ones who tell you that you can't do this, can't do that, the ones who tell you that your dreams are just childhood fantasies that you'll never be able to accomplish. They may not mean to be harmful. They may be well intentioned and might not even know they're doing it. But their negativity is a poison to everyone around them, polluting the atmosphere, coloring everything. They are the Fellowship of the Miserable, and they are the killers of the dream.

We must understand what negative people do. Not only do they tend to create an environment that pervades the mood of everyone around them, they also are usually the worst role models you can have. Negative people usually surrender during adversity. They look for reasons why things won't work, rather than explore why they *will* work. They look for things to blame. They are more prone to use excuses. They are the first to complain when things aren't going right, the first to doubt. They are more prone to failure.

So you must find a way to fight through their negativity, because they try to suck the air out of everyone. You must find a way to block out that negativity.

Because you have a right to be happy, a right not to be brought down by the people around you.

So how do you fight through the negativity that's all around you? How do you deal with disruptive people in the workplace, the people who take away from your own ability to achieve success, as well as the group's?

You must confront them.

The simplest way is to let those people know face-to-face that their behavior is bothering you and how much they could help the group if they acted in a more positive manner. Going behind such a person's back and complaining about him or her is merely wasting energy, and is ultimately self-defeating. Odds are it will only make that person more of a distraction, and you, too, would be brought down to his or her level.

The best way to deal with disruptive people is to point out to them that they have much to contribute to the overall climate of the workplace, but their negativity is affecting everyone. This may not instantly cure the situation, but at least they are going to know their behavior is upsetting others. At the very least that's a starting point for them to think about changing their behavior.

If this fails, there are other avenues that can be explored. Sometimes it might be giving the negative person a book or a magazine article—anything you can think of—to get him or her to look at things differently and have a change in attitude.

Or else maybe you can find someone in the workplace he or she either likes or admires who will talk to this person about the negative behavior.

Obviously, there is only so much you can do.

But you can keep the negativity from rubbing off on you. Surround yourself with positive people, positive influences, and concentrate on not letting a cynical attitude creep into your life. This is easier said than done, of course. It must be practiced, it must be preached, it must be part of your daily diet, because negative behavior is always around you to some extent. Again, this becomes another matter of your discipline. For you must keep fighting off all those negative viruses that always will be swirling around you.

Then there are the social distractions. They are different from negative people, but potentially just as lethal. If you let them, the social distractions will get in the way of overachieving as surely as clouds get in the way of the sun. It's the people who want to talk at work. The friends who want you to take the afternoon off and play golf. The friends who tell you to relax, that you're working too hard. The people who call you a workaholic and tell you to lighten up.

These are the social distractions, and they, too, get in the way of your reaching your full potential. You simply must minimize the time you spend with these people. *True* friends would never want to get in the way of your goals, and they will understand when you have to say no. As for the people who use you just to have something to do, you need to seriously consider whether you can afford to have these people in your life.

## STAYING POSITIVE IN DIFFICULT TIMES

Change is something that happens to all of us as we move through life.

We all must constantly adapt to new circumstances and very often it's our ability to handle change that determines the quality of our lives.

This is especially important in the workplace, where every day brings changes in the marketplace in technologies and in organizational structure, whether it's downsizing, re-alignment, or changing strategies as companies begin looking toward the next century.

Once upon a time we all thought that a work situation was forever. The company was always going to be there; you were always going to have a job. Well, what was true for most is now unheard of for almost all of us. Everything is in flux, and you have to be able to handle it.

Change is not knowing what's going to happen. That's all it is.

Yet so many people fear change. The very idea of change makes them uncomfortable.

Why?

Because they essentially are looking at things with the wrong attitude. The unspoken assumption is *that change is going to be for the worse*. The unspoken assumption is that change is a negative.

It's like traveling through a tunnel. Positive people will tell themselves that at the other end of the tunnel there might be some hidden treasure that can help lead them to greatness. Negative people will see that same tunnel and say that at the end of that tunnel it might be dark or something evil. It's all about attitude.

You have to look at change as something that's exciting, something that's valuable. People with high self-esteem and passion will look at change as being stimulating and exciting, enabling them to conquer new horizons, instead of something that's going to inhibit them and make them nervous, apprehensive about both their job and their confidence in themselves.

The positive person looks at change as opportunity.

I have had ten of my former assistant coaches go on to become head coaches, something I take a great deal of pride in. And one of the things I always ask them when they come to me for advice on whether they should take the job is can they win there?

That's the question.

I don't ask how much money they would be making. I learned a long time ago that you should never chase money; that if you chase winning, the money will chase you. But can you win? Can you be successful?

That is how we must look at change.

As an opportunity.

As a chance to be more successful.

And the only way to do that is by being positive. By looking at a situation and putting a positive spin on it instead of a negative one. By looking at a situation and seeing its potential for you. For you have to be able to take the rough moments in life and be able to shrink them down.

You also must understand that every day is not going to be wine and roses. We all face pitfalls on a daily basis. How we minimize those and maximize the good times is what's crucial. That is where your attitude keeps everything on the upswing. That's what we're striving for: to be on the upswing as much as possible.

So when you feel yourself going into a negative mood, you have to stop yourself and get yourself out of that downward cycle. First, you have to recognize why you're down. What's getting you frustrated? Is it the circumstances? Or is it just a fear of not knowing the circumstances? What's affecting your mood?

Then you have to admit the obvious to yourself: These mood swings are not going to benefit you in any way whatsoever. Just the opposite.

These mood swings are destructive. They are only hurting you, both on a personal level and in how others perceive you. Once you recognize and admit that you can start to put more positive forces in motion.

## THE PRECIOUS PRESENT

Every year I start off our first practice by gathering my players around me and telling them a terrific and meaningful story.

I read them a little book called *The Precious Present* by a man named Spencer Johnson. It takes only about five minutes.

The story is about a little boy, an old man, and the wisdom that comes with age.

"You have a great gift," the old man tells the boy. "It's called the precious present, and it's the best present a person can receive because anyone who receives such a gift is happy forever."

"Wow!" the little boy said. "I hope someone gives me the precious present. Maybe I'll get it for Christmas."

The old man smiled as the little boy ran off to play. The little boy was always happy, whistling, and smiling as he worked and played.

As the years passed, the boy would approach the old man and asked him again and again about the precious present. After all, the boy knew about toys. So why couldn't he figure out what the precious present was? It had to be something special, he knew, because the old man had said it would bring happiness forever.

"Is it a magical thing?" he asked.

"No," the old man said.

"A flying carpet?"

"No," the old man quietly replied.

"Sunken treasure left by pirates?" the boy asked. He was now getting older and felt uncomfortable asking. Still, he wanted to know. He *had* to know.

Finally, the boy, now a young man, became annoyed.

"You told me," he said, "that anyone who receives such a present would be happy forever. I never got such a gift as a child."

"I'm afraid you don't understand," the old man said.

"If you want me to be happy," the young man shouted, "why don't you just tell me what the precious present is?"

"And where to find it?" the old man said. "I would like to, but I do not have such power. No one does. Only you have the power to make yourself happy. Only you."

The young man left, packed his bags, and began a life-long quest for the precious present. He looked everywhere, in caves, jungles, underneath the seas. He read books, looked in the mirror, studied the faces of other people.

But he never found the precious present.

Finally, after many years, when he became an old man, it hit him what the precious present is. It is just that: The Present. Not the past and not the future, but the precious present.

It's not a toy. It's not a gift.

It's the ability to live in the present tense.

This is such an important lesson for all of us today.

We are so concerned with what people say and with what people are thinking of us. We become obsessed with a loss or a failure and let it consume us. We become focused on yesterday and the mistakes of the past.

Well, yesterday's problems are just that—yesterday's.

They are a done deal. There's nothing you can do about the day that's over except learn from your mistakes.

And if it isn't the past, we are stressed about the future.

What's going to happen to our job?

Is it even going to be there a year from now?

What's going to happen if it's not?

We have all woken up in the middle of the night feeling anxious about what the future might bring. It's part of human nature. But this kind of worry never gets us anywhere, except making us sick and tired. We have to learn to minimize these times, not let them take over our psyche and shove out productive thoughts.

I want my players to live in the precious present. And I want to live there too. To both coach and live like every day is my last, not taking anything for granted. In our anxious society, this is a hard thing to do. But we can all look around us to see how anxious thoughts keep people from acting while life passes them by. We have to remember that this can happen to us, too. We have to sit back at times and become totally immersed in the moment. You would be amazed how simply concentrating on a task, apart from worry or regret, can be a gratifying, peaceful, positive experience.

## Key Points for Step 3

You can condition yourself to be more positive. Being positive isn't an unattainable state. It is an attitude, and attitudes can be worked on. You control both your attitude and your mood.

You must block out the negativity that's around you. You do this by realizing that the negative people around you are an incredible drain on your desire to be more successful. Surround yourself with positive people and the benefits will rub off on you.

△

The more trying the times the more positive you must be. You must adapt to change, and condition yourself to see it as an opportunity to improve yourself, not as a window to failure.

△

Learning to live in the present tense—one that's free from the failures of the past and the anxieties of the future—is a wonderful gift, and one you always should be striving for.

# POSITIVE ATTITUDE
# COMES FROM LOVE
# AND RESPECT

I tell people that Rick Pitino is the best psychologist I've known. The reason why I say this is because he takes the time to really get to know his players. It's not superficial, or false knowledge. He really knows them, knows what it takes to make them tick. He is a master of understanding each player's strength and weaknesses and then going about the process of maximizing their strengths while minimizing their weaknesses.

Rick's extremely honest when he discusses strengths and weaknesses with a player. I've seen him with different individuals, and he's brutally honest with them whatever the weakness may be. Although he's very honest with them, he always makes sure that they leave with their heads up. He never leaves them on the floor. People appreciate that honesty, rather than being left to wonder what the other person is really thinking. With Rick, his players always know not only where they stand but what the situation is. There are no doubts, no gray areas.

A good example of this is how he's handled Nazr Mohammed, a

sophomore from Chicago, a player with a lot of potential but who was very raw when he first arrived.

Rick is very tough on Nazr, but always in a positive way. He'll literally talk Nazr through the play, making certain Nazr knows what's going on. It's Rick's way of building confidence in that young man.

I've learned a great deal in terms of motivational skills by watching and observing Rick. I can't begin to tell you how impressed I am.

I feel he has the real key to good discipline. Rick lets his players know when he is disappointed with them, that they have let him down. They see it, understand it, and that makes them feel bad. As a result, they are willing to go that extra mile in order to please him. That's the greatest way to discipline: the pain they get from knowing they've disappointed him becomes the discipline.

I've seen him use that method with his own sons. They'll do something wrong, and when they see the disappointment in his eyes, when they see they've let him down, he doesn't even have to say a word to make them feel remorse. That's discipline.

But that method can only work if the one being disciplined—whether it's the player or child—know that behind it all is both love and respect for them. Rick's players know that he loves them like family. That's the one principle that underlies everything.

Father Ed Bradley
HENDERSON, KY

# STEP 4 ESTABLISH GOOD HABITS

H abit, as defined by *Webster*'s, is "the tendency or disposition to act in a certain way, acquired by repetition of such acts."

This does not say we're born with good habits or bad habits; it simply means that we've repeated a specific action enough times that it begins to look like instinct. It means that this behavior has become reinforced in our heads and in our bodies so often that it has become second nature.

This is good news and bad news.

Habits develop consistency. But consistency can either work in our favor or work against us. Repetition of bad habits defeats our purpose and keeps us from achieving excellence. The golfer who goes out and constantly works on a swing that's full of flaws is certainly not executing good habits. He may think he's helping himself get better as a golfer by putting in so much practice time, but he's deluding himself. All he's doing is reinforcing incorrect behavior that will eventually become second nature.

People in the workplace who develop a reputation for always looking for the easy way out are all but signing their own death sentence as far as advancement in their companies goes. It might not be anything overt, like continually being late and failing to meet performance standards. It might be infinitely more subtle, like conveying to management that although the job is important, it's not life and death, not a passion. It might be small things, like being the first person out the door at five o'clock or never coming in early to get work done before the boss is in. It might be never volunteering for anything extra. It might be not having enough of a positive attitude.

Again, the above might not be major offenses when you take a look at each one individually, and sometimes people might not even know they are sending out these messages.

But these are all bad habits.

We see bad habits all around us all the time. One example might be the person in an exercise routine who takes a day off when he doesn't feel like working out, telling himself he'll make it up the next day by working doubly hard. Not a major offense, certainly. But string a few of those days together and that well-intentioned exercise plan isn't worth anything.

Or the student who puts off doing her homework until late at night and then often feels too tired to finish it, telling herself that she'll finish it during study hall the next morning. Or the salesperson who immediately goes home after he or she meets the day's quota.

What is a bad habit?

That's simple.

A bad habit is any habit that doesn't serve you in a positive way. It's also the act of repeating something over and over in the wrong way—bad repetitions.

Let's examine other common bad habits in the workplace.

One is distractions. These can be many things. It's making personal calls that drag on too long. It's the conversation at the coffee machine that goes on past the second cup of coffee. It's the social interruptions that cut into everyone's productivity. In other words, saying hello and good-bye shouldn't be taking up an hour of your day.

Another is excuses. This is the attitude that says, "Yes, I may be wasting too much time during the day having social conversations and killing time by the coffee machine, but everyone does that." "Yes, I may be all but running for the door at five o'clock, but so is everybody else." "Yes, I may not exactly be devoting myself to my job, but no one else is either."

A third is being on time. That's right. Being on time at work is a bad habit. It can't be a good habit, because being on time is a given. An athlete, however, wouldn't think of showing up for an eight o'clock game at seven fifty-five and then just going out to play without stretching and doing the proper warm-up. A professional golfer doesn't get out of his car and walk to the first tee. A singer doesn't simply walk out on the stage and launch into a song without doing the proper voice exercises.

So why should someone who is going to work at the appointed hour think that he or she is fully prepared for the day?

What you should be doing is arriving at work a half hour early and getting all of your social conversations out of the way, getting your newspaper read, and getting your coffee poured, so that when the workday starts you are ready. You need this time to prepare so that by the time you start, you're mentally at the top of your game. You should be ready to work once the workday starts, not just starting to get adjusted.

It's what I'm constantly telling my team all the time: When they step between the lines at practice they must give their full attention for two hours. It's the same for you at work. When the workday is in progress that should be where all your energy is focused. If you want to socialize with co-workers, that should come after work.

Another bad habit is wasting too much energy on things in the workplace that you cannot control, whether it's being envious of co-workers or being critical about them. Gossip is a common practice in virtually every workplace there is, and it's not only self-defeating, it's a waste of time. Usually, this is all out of your control anyway and not worthy of both the time and the energy you give to it.

A fifth common bad habit is allowing your personal life to come into the workplace. This happens all the time, and it's potentially very destructive. You can't keep bringing your personal life to the workplace without eventually paying a price for it, either by losing your focus on the work at hand or having co-workers start to talk about your life. Invariably, once the word gets out that you're having personal problems, they get exaggerated and spread like wildfire.

That's the problem with bad habits. They spread. They get magnified. Eventually, they get noticed, like the guy who comes to work with two different-colored socks.

These are all bad habits, and you can learn an important lesson from all of them. You can have the best intentions in the world. You can work hard and be disciplined. You can put in long hours. You can have good self-esteem and a positive attitude, too. You can think you're doing everything in your power to be more successful. But if you are only reinforcing bad habits then it's all counterproductive.

So when you discover a bad habit you must do what is

necessary to break it. You must also do this as quickly as possible, because bad habits get harder to correct the more entrenched they become. If you look at any list of successful people—men and women who have been winners—you'll invariably find they reached the top because they developed good habits, then used them to their advantage. All too often the line between success and failure is very slight, very tenuous. By making a habit of doing things right, you increase the odds you can be more successful on a consistent basis.

As a coach, I've come to understand that the old adage "Practice makes perfect" is slightly off the mark.

*Perfect practice makes perfect.* That's the key.

Proper fundamentals are necessary to developing good habits. Then we must repeat an act in the proper way in order to form habits that are sound fundamentally. That's called repetition, and repetition is the key to success. Create good solid habits, then repeat them over and over until they become so natural they become second nature. This is the discipline that's such an integral part of deserving victory. This is the only way to sustain a high level of excellence.

Whether the challenge is to develop better speech patterns or a better golf swing or a better attitude, the solution is the same: Establish the proper techniques, work tirelessly on improving them, and without question you will get better at what you're working at. It all comes down to having a solid foundation on which to build.

One of the highest compliments you can give anyone in any workplace is to call them a pro, regardless of his or her occupation. Just what does that mean? Simply, that the person comes to work every day and does his or her job to the best of his or her ability. This person is not distracted. The pro doesn't turn it on and off. The pro's energy level doesn't waver from one day to the next. The pro doesn't have a lot of mood shifts that affect his or her performance. This person always gives a good performance, day after day, week after week. That's what being a pro is all about, and that's what you should be striving for.

Good habits are the way you do this.

Good habits also are a safeguard against underachieving. They prevent laziness. They prevent floundering. They prevent listlessness. Good habits create organization and discipline in our lives. It's virtually impossible to achieve success without having good habits, virtually impossible to reach your full potential. And in times of stress, times when you are being severely tested, good habits become even more important. They become the rock, the standard of behavior that we must stick with so that we don't get off track.

I learned this early in life.

I first picked up a basketball when I was seven years old, and that was probably an accident. You see, my family had little interest in sports. My father, who managed a building in Manhattan, played a little handball and my older brothers, Bob and Ron, played a little football, but none of them were big sports fans. We were living in Cambria Heights, Queens, although I had been born in Manhattan and had spent the first few years of my life just a few blocks away from Madison Square Garden.

Now I was young, but I really wanted to be good at something. I learned my work ethic from my father, who got up at five-thirty every morning. And I learned how to be organized from my mother, who was the glue that kept my family together. But the fact that I found that basketball is what I wanted to devote myself to happened just by chance. One day I was at the playground with my cousin Walter Bachman, who is a few years older than I am, and he suggested that I try out for the team at Sacred Heart School. "All you have to do is be able to make a lay-up and they'll put you on the team," he said.

"What's a lay-up?" I asked.

Walter showed me how to do it, how to go off my left foot and shoot the ball off the backboard with my right hand. After he left that afternoon, I stayed at the playground and practiced the shot by myself until I was able to make a lay-up. The next day I made the team.

I was never the most gifted kid athletically. I couldn't jump all that well. I didn't have blinding speed or great size. I knew from an early age that if I was ever going to be the kind of basketball player I wanted to be I was going to have to work at it, that there was going to be no other way. I was willing to do that, so I learned very early the importance of a strong work ethic.

I learned two valuable things that first day in the playground, even if I probably didn't realize their significance at the time. I learned that you must have the right techniques and that you must be willing to work at them. And I learned that if you do these things, you can reach your goals. Just think how much easier it could be for so many children if they could learn that simple lesson I learned that day: *The right technique plus practice helps you reach your goals.*

How do you establish good habits?

Here are some ways.

## ORGANIZE YOUR DAY AND YOUR ACTIONS

What do you want to accomplish during this day?

Are you trying to be the best parent you can be? The best salesperson? Are you trying to be the best teacher or run the best small business? What are you trying to be?

You open your eyes with a purpose. The day is not just something that happens to you, some wave that rolls over you and tosses you in any direction it wants. The day is not just some overwhelming force that you're powerless against. The day is something you can control, something on which you can exert your will and your discipline.

Every day you must have a systematic plan and set specific goals. You should decide what you want to accomplish and determine what methods you're going to use. You start the day with a purpose; you end the day with your accomplishments.

And you write this purpose down on paper.

One secret to success I've learned the hard way is incredibly basic: Write everything down. Leave nothing to memory. Memory gets you in trouble. Memory ultimately betrays you. Memory allows you to be unfocused. Memory gives you an easy excuse when you fail.

So every morning I write down my goals for the day. This list of goals becomes my plan. And although it certainly can be altered as the events of the day occur, it provides my working outline. Just as you need a plan in life, you also need one for each day, each week, each month, each year. That's the only way you logically can progress toward your long-term goals.

Writing down your day's purpose simply makes you better organized.

I also carry around index cards, on which I'm forever jotting ideas down and making notes to myself. This is another way of being better organized and prepared to remember things you will need to refer back to later.

Being organized is having that plan of attack I keep talking about. Defining your day's purpose leaves you with no excuses. You don't get sidetracked, you don't forget. Many people wake up with goals for the day; but the goals are vague and unfocused, thus easy to dismiss or leave behind as the day goes along. But once you have a tangible list, you can then develop the methods you're going to use to make those purposes stand up during the day. And after the day is over, you can sit down and list what you have accomplished.

Just as important, though, is listing the things you failed to accomplish and the reasons why. What got in the way? Were you unprepared? Were you needlessly distracted? Could it have been rectified?

By making a daily plan you are instantly imposing some discipline on your time, and your actions. You lead the day rather than letting it be swept away from you. Day by day you are taking more control of your life. But the plan is also useful for exposing the weak links you had that day. You can have a reckoning with yourself about the small things you weren't able to accomplish that day rather than letting them all pile up somewhere down the road.

Self-motivated people do these things every day. Not once in a while. Not only when they're feeling exceptionally energetic. Not only when they're feeling guilty that they're drifting back into the same old bad habits they're trying to change. Every day.

Not that this is easy. Especially for people who don't get a lot of support, whether it's the saleswoman on the road by herself or the father who is trying to be a more successful parent.

Understand, though, that making a plan is a significant beginning. The very act of defining your purpose for each day—stating in black and white what you want to accomplish— quickly makes you a more focused person. String enough days together and you have a week. String four weeks together and you have a month. String four months together and you have a different person.

Now you must understand that there are always going to be distractions, so you must also be aware of their warning signs: the day starting to slip by you, interruptions to your work flow, procrastinations. More things that keep getting put off mean more chances you have of getting sidetracked from your goals.

But if you're an organized person, you plan to be distracted and you have strategies to compensate for it. One way to minimize this is to rise early and start your day. Our days get more and more cluttered as they progress, but there usually is very little clutter early in the morning.

Take exercise, for example, something we will talk about later in this chapter as an important way to establish discipline in your life and raise self-esteem. But when do you do it? If you schedule it for the evening, when work is over, it's very likely your day will get away from you and you will run out of time. So schedule it early in the day.

It's a lesson for anything you consider important.

## DON'T PUT THINGS OFF

When I go to work in the morning, things I don't like to do I do right away.

If I have to make two or three unpleasant phone calls over the course of a day I always try to make them early on. By getting these done right away you are able to put a positive spin on the rest of your day. By postponing them they hang over your head like a guillotine, putting a negative spin on everything you do before you bite the bullet and make those calls. The rule should be simple: If we have twelve hours in the day and eight are going to be enjoyable and four are not, let's get those four out of the way as quickly as possible.

For instance, if you have a dentist appointment that's potentially unpleasant, schedule it for as early in the day as possible. That way you get it out of the way and you can enjoy the rest of the day. If you schedule that appointment for late in the day, you'll probably spend most of the day thinking about it, worrying about it. Your anticipation only makes it worse.

Remember what we talked about in Step 2, "Set Demanding Goals"?: Hard work isn't always fun, and there are going to be a lot of things that crop up during the day and during the week that are not particularly fun. You are always going to have goals to accomplish, which sometimes feel like ten-foot hurdles you have to somehow get over. There'll always be things you'd rather avoid and postpone to some undetermined time. The trick is not to put these tasks off. Not to postpone them until tomorrow. This is how bad habits get reinforced. What you have to do is make yourself do these things first.

The rule is simple: Anything you consider unpleasant do first. Get it behind you.

## GET YOURSELF IN SHAPE

When you read the words above, I know what you were thinking: "I'm not trying to make the team at Kentucky; I'm not trying to be an athlete. So why is being in great shape so important?"

Simple.

You are trying to achieve more. You are trying to be more successful in whatever your individual arena is. You are trying not only to reach your potential but to move beyond it. To overachieve. So don't fool yourself.

As we talked about in the introduction, "Deserving Victory," this takes great effort. A good old-fashioned work ethic. To maintain this work ethic, you not only must be in the best possible health you can be but must have stamina and perseverance and other traits of mental toughness, which are easier to have if you're in good shape. You have to want to get up the next day. You have to get up in the morning feeling good about yourself and the opportunity of the day ahead. You have to be able to sustain a high degree of energy throughout the day. If you are not in the best shape you can be, these things simply become more difficult to achieve.

And this is even more true the older you become.

We all know that as companies downsize and streamline, older workers are often targeted. You must also understand there's sometimes a prejudice in the workplace against workers who are not in the age range of twenty to thirty-five years. Why? Invariably, it's because employers don't think an employee's energy level is the same at fifty as it is at thirty-five. They think older people have lost some of that passion, that eye-of-the-tiger attitude.

So you must do everything—both through your appearance and your attitude—to overcome this prejudice. You have wisdom and experience. Everyone knows that. That's one of the pluses of age. Now you must prove you can work long hours. You have to prove you still have the drive to excel. You have to prove you still have passion and a high energy level. And to do that, you must be in the best shape you can be in.

It's important, then, that you make exercise a part of your daily routine.

Don't tell me you don't have the time.

Make the time.

You make the time to eat, don't you? You make the time to sleep, don't you? So make the time for some kind of exercise routine. It doesn't have to be anything arduous. It doesn't have to be the type of regimen that's going to give you a chance to be on the next Olympic team.

The first thing I try to do every day is exercise, usually right after I rise. My goal is to get some form of aerobic workout. It doesn't take long: usually fifteen to twenty minutes, maximum.

Just do something.

Whether it's going to a gym, doing aerobics in your living room, or just walking around the block—make the effort.

And try to do it every day. Besides being good for you, it will start to raise your self-esteem and make you feel better about yourself. It's another important building block in putting discipline into your life. It puts you in the frame of mind necessary to achieve success.

## MAKING A GREAT FIRST IMPRESSION

Your appearance is important.

This does not mean making a fashion statement or appearing on any best-dressed list. You should simply try to capture the essence of being organized.

Right or wrong, a good appearance inspires trust in the people who deal with you. It's the old truth that people don't invest their money with someone who locks sloppy and undisciplined. There are reasons why bankers don't wear warm-up suits to work and why people don't go on job interviews with their shirts hanging out. How you look, how you dress, how well groomed you are, are often the first impressions anyone has of you. Even though these factors may be shallow and misleading.

How you dress is your perception of yourself, and you should never forget for a second that people form opinions of you based on that.

What you're trying to do, then, is make a habit out of being physically and mentally ready to make a great first impression. That's the goal here: to present yourself in the best possible light, like an actor who insists on being photographed from the right angle. What you should be trying to accomplish is to come across as yourself, while also giving off the impression that you have your act together, that you are someone with discipline.

It's also critical that you always look your best, and not just on a formal job interview. Because you never know when someone's watching you and forming a first impression. This happens all the time. People see you in certain situations and make judgments about you based on very little knowledge: what you wear, how you act, how you carry yourself, what attitude you convey.

Some of this, obviously, might be very misleading, and people might eventually end up with a much different impression of you once they get to know you. Unfortunately, too often you don't have that luxury. All of us are frequently judged quickly and by superficial criteria. That's just the way it is, and you have to deal with that reality. So you must always be conscious of being on guard—what we in sports call "being on your game"—for you never know when you might miss an opportunity.

## YOU CAN NEVER BE OVERPREPARED

In my early days of recruiting I often would go into a recruit's home without knowing a lot about him. At the time I figured that I didn't really have to know a lot about him, his family, or their agenda, that the force and power of my presentation would be enough to convince that recruit to come to my school.

Was that foolish?

No question.

But it's a mistake people make all the time. We meet someone who, we hope, can help us in business yet we know nothing about that person. We go on job interviews and don't know enough about the company we want to be hired by. We think about working in certain professions, yet know little about how they operate. In short, we don't do the necessary research that might give us that little edge.

We don't need to do research only when we are trying to sell someone something, or convince people of something. We need to be researching all the time to keep getting better at what we do.

When I give a motivational speech to a company—which I do approximately thirty times a year—I try to find out as much about that company as I can. What are its strengths? What are its weaknesses? What are its specific problems? What are its goals? Where does it want to go? The more information I can garner about that company, the better the speech I can give to the employees.

No sports team—at any level—would go out and play a game without some knowledge of its opponent. It's called scouting, and everyone does it for one simple reason: It gives you an advantage to know as much about your opponent as possible. And the higher you go up the ladder in sports the more sophisticated scouting your opponent becomes. At Kentucky, we want to know everything we can about our opponent. What offenses do they run? What defenses? What is their line-up? What are their tendencies late in games? And our opponents want to know the same things about us.

If this is so important in the competitive nature of sports, doesn't it make sense that it applies in other areas of life too?

You always have to keep studying, keep learning, keep discovering how you can get an edge. Constantly try to ask how you can do it better.

Get into the habit of seeking out new educational tools—whether it's taking classes at night or reading more industry journals or learning a new computer system. Self-education is a constant means to survival in the workplace, to keeping up with new trends and technologies, especially in today's business climate. You can't create the perception you are content with your knowledge base. Things are moving too quickly. You must do everything in your power to keep up. If you don't, you are all but hanging a sign around your neck and labeling yourself as obsolete.

It's an old saying, but it's as true as ever: You can't be too prepared.

When a young basketball player named Jamal Mashburn was in high school in New York City, his reputation was of a lazy, overweight young man who didn't play hard. I had people telling me we shouldn't recruit him, that even though he was very talented, he never would be able to play in a program as demanding as ours.

The first thing I did was do a little research, wanting to find out as much as I could about Jamal before we actually met. I discovered that he was only sixteen; no wonder everyone kept saying he was immature. I also learned he had never trained extensively. His body was soft and underdeveloped, and he wasn't in great shape, which no doubt contributed to his inability to play hard.

When I first met him, I said, "Jamal, I have a reputation for overworking my players and you have a reputation for being lazy and not wanting to work hard. Why would you possibly want to play for me?"

"I want to be a professional ballplayer," he answered, "and I know that in order to get there I'm going to have to work hard. You'll make me do that."

After that I knew I would have no problem with Jamal, because I knew I had someone who was willing to work hard. Not that Jamal ever really liked working hard. He had to be pushed. He had to be prodded. But he had a dream, and he was willing to do what it took to achieve it. He knew it was a means to an end.

So Jamal succeeded—and so did I. Without a little homework, I'm sure the outcome would have been very different.

The lesson here is we never can do too much homework, never can be overprepared. Especially in today's changing workplace.

We are all fortunate in one respect. Modern technology has made it easier for us to develop good habits. From a coaching standpoint I can tell you it's been a real blessing. No longer can my players doubt or argue with what I and my assistant coaches tell them or argue with us. Let's say there's a flaw in a player's jump-shot. It's right there on the film. We can show it to the player, point out what he's doing wrong, then help him begin the process of developing the mechanics that will enable him to overcome his flaw

This same process can be used in a multitude of ways, whether it's practicing your ability to speak in public or even how you address your children. With the technology available today you have the means to see yourself on tape, compare it to the model you're trying to emulate, and see how close you come to replicating it. The technology is available. It's up to you to take advantage of it and make it work for you.

There are endless ways you can better prepare yourself for what you have to do. If you're pitching a service to a new client, find out what made him or her dissatisfied with the old order. If you're presenting a solution to a business problem to your boss, have a Plan B and a Plan X ready just in case.

It's all part of being prepared, and being prepared does several things: It keeps you up to date in the marketplace; it makes you more of a commodity in the workplace; it makes you better at what you do, regardless of what it is; and it gives you the confidence you need to succeed.

You know you're prepared, thus you know you're ready for whatever obstacle comes along. You've established good habits. You always are doing your homework. You're constantly trying to learn more and increase your knowledge base. It's time to take on the world.

## Key Points for Step 4

With good habits, success becomes second nature. Don't let bad habits make it easy to fail. You must have a purpose for each day. This gives each day a structure and the sense you are controlling the day and not being controlled by it. Purpose establishes your discipline and makes you more focused.

△

Don't put things off. Get in the habit every day of doing the more unpleasant things first. This not only eliminates the stress but leaves the rest of the day for more pleasant things.

Get your mind and body ready for success. Ninety percent of the time first impressions are the ones that last. Don't force people to require a second meeting to find out who you are.

Do your homework. Your competitor is.

# THERE ARE NO DAYS
# OFF IN LIFE

The main thing about Rick is his ability to motivate on a daily basis.

There are people who give great speeches, who aren't necessarily great motivators. But having been around Rick with the New York Knicks and here at the University of Kentucky, it's what he does every single day that's so impressive. There are no off-days with Rick. There are no days when he puts things off until tomorrow.

A good example is when we were with the Knicks. As assistant coaches, Stu Jackson and I had the job of stealing the calls that both the opposing coach and opposing point guard tried to make. We would try to steal them and then let our players know what plays the other team was trying to run.

One night—I can't remember the specific opponent—we had stolen something like sixty-seven out of sixty-eight plays the other team ran. After the game Stu and I were happy about that, having got every play except one. We got in the locker room and Rick wanted to know how we had missed the one.

"Were you guys in a coma or what?" he asked.

We were surprised, but we came to understand the standard Rick had for trying to win a basketball game. We were all going to try to do everything we could do to best prepare our team to win, and there was never going to be a time when we were going to rest or be happy with anything except excellence.

It's a lesson that I learned from Rick, and it's an invaluable one.

The best definition of excellence I've ever heard is this: "Excellence is the unlimited ability to improve the quality of what you have to offer."

That's Rick.

He exemplifies that on a daily basis. He never believes he has all the answers. Nor does he believe the people around him, or his organization, have achieved enough. As a result he's always looking—on an almost daily basis—for ways to improve.

Every day before practice Rick meets with our players. He talks to them from anywhere from a minute to ten minutes on what it is that they can do to improve themselves, and why it's so important for them to improve themselves. During one of those sessions he came in and read the whole book *The Precious Present* and then quizzed them on what the "precious present" was. He really talked to them that day, and for a number of days afterward, about how important it is for individuals who are interested in achievement to dwell in the present, to not look back to the past and to not really worry that much about the future. Rather, he told them to deal with the present, to work hardest on the given day you have in front of you. And if they did work hard, the result will be that things will turn out for the best.

Rick not only truly believes this, he lives it. It's what makes him a daily motivator.

He doesn't wait for the future to motivate the people around him. He doesn't say that they were motivated enough in the past. As a leader, the head of our organization, his viewpoint is, "How can I lift people today?" And he never misses an opportunity to lift them up on a daily basis, myself included.

Jim O'Brien
UNIVERSITY OF KENTUCKY ASSOCIATE COACH

# STEP 5

## MASTER THE ART OF COMMUNICATION

One skill we should all cultivate further is effective communication. Communicating clearly—to your boss, employers, co-workers, friends, children, spouse—is a critical part of your success and your ability to improve the conditions you live and work in. Many people think that good communicators are born, not made, and that some people are just naturally good speakers and motivators. They think the rest of us are, well, just destined to sit on the sidelines.

Untrue.

Communication is a habit, just like the other ones we've talked about. And being a habit, it can be learned and mastered. It is such an important habit, in fact, that it deserves its own step, its own place on the path to success.

It's also a little different. Unlike the other good habits you are trying to establish, this one is not just about self-directed control and inner focus. When there is only one person to worry about—yourself—it's easier to commit to working hard and controlling how well you can perform. But communication is interaction outside yourself, with other people, and about the ability to gauge a situation so that you convey the right thing at the right time.

Life is about dealing with other people: those above us (our boss), those around us (our colleagues and friends), and those who look up to us (our employees and children). The art of communication is about how to make contact with each of these groups so that they can help you achieve your goals, and you, in turn, can help them achieve theirs. For even though you are on the road to self-improvement, it's not a journey you're taking in a vacuum.

If you can't communicate with people, you have dramatically narrowed your chances for success.

In basketball, if you can't communicate with your players, you can take all your strategies, all your thought-out philosophies, all your hard work, and throw them in the nearest trash can. You just aren't going to be successful. The same thing is true in business, yet it's amazing how many managers don't communicate their goals and their company's goals. Invariably, in failing to communicate these goals, managers end up creating more problems for themselves.

Effective communication is the best problem solver there is, but so many of us don't know how to go about it. We talk and talk, but we don't communicate and we don't establish that connection. All too often, we have a discussion with someone that leads to a debate that leads to an argument that then leads to a break in trust. Then we either dismiss that person or exclude them from our lives.

Why?

Because of a failure to communicate.

Never underestimate just how important that personal connection is.

Case in point:

When I was coaching the Knicks I had a player named Bill Cartwright, who had really begun playing very well for us. His confidence was sky high, even though he didn't feel good about himself at the start of the season, because he figured that he wasn't in our plans and that we were going to trade him. But his self-esteem had improved dramatically and now his self-confidence was soaring.

One day we were to play the Chicago Bulls, and he called in sick for the morning "shoot-around." This is a light practice on the day of a game in which professional teams go over scouting reports for the upcoming game and just generally work out the kinks.

I was concerned about Bill's health because we had a difficult stretch coming up and we needed him to be successful. So I told the trainer to call Bill and make sure he saw a doctor. I figured that he might have to miss that night's game against the Bulls; but by seeing a doctor right away and getting the proper medical attention, he would get back to us as soon as possible.

Sounds simple, right?

It should have been.

But because I didn't call him myself— a call that probably would have taken me two minutes—the whole situation became convoluted.

Billy's response to the trainer, who told Billy that I wanted him to go to the doctor, was, "Doesn't Rick think I'm sick? I don't feel well enough to leave the house today."

The trainer said he didn't know anything about that and just stressed that I had said that Billy had better see a doctor.

What I should have done was call Billy myself and tell him my concern about his health. I should have let him know that because he was so valuable to our team, I wanted him to come back as soon as he was up to it. If I had done that, everything would have been fine. Instead, by going through a third person my message had been misinterpreted, and Billy thought I was questioning his integrity. He believed that I felt that he was just trying to get out of that morning's shootaround, a practice that many of the veteran players see as essentially pointless, unnecessary drudgery. But I didn't know any of this. I simply thought that the matter had been handled. When Billy came back to practice the next week, there was a change in the way he dealt with me. Our relationship had become strained.

Still, I didn't address the situation. I just let it continue to take its own course. Finally, though, I had had enough of the uncomfortable feelings and said to the Knicks' doctor, "I can't believe what's happening with Cartwright's attitude. There must be something wrong in his personal life."

He said, "Don't you know?"

"Not at all," I said.

"He thinks you don't trust him," the doctor said. "That you thought he was faking about his illness."

I was stunned. I said that hadn't been the case at all.

"Did you tell Billy that?" asked the doctor.

"No," I said. "I told the trainer to tell him."

I had completely overlooked how much my player needed approval from me—implicit approval that could only come from my personally reaching out.

After that, I got a lot smarter in a hurry. I met with Cartwright, told him what had happened, and apologized for not calling him myself, and that was it. Billy understood, instantly felt better, and our relationship returned to what it had been before the incident.

And what had I learned?

Several lessons about how communication is so important.

For one, here was something that on the surface seemed to be a minor incident, a simple case of misunderstanding, but this miscommunication had the potential to change an entire relationship.

Second, any time you go through someone else to get your message across, there's potential for a problem. This was brought home to me hard, so now I always try to call someone myself and not ask my secretary or one of my assistant coaches to do it for me. The rule? Do it yourself. The person you're calling will appreciate it, and things won't get misinterpreted.

The third lesson? Don't let things fester. By not dealing with the situation once I sensed something was different about Cartwright, I had only made things worse.

A fourth lesson: What you don't say can have as great an impact as the things you do say.

And I thought I was a good communicator.

Communication is something I always studied, ever since I knew I wanted to one day be a coach. I used to listen to tapes of Martin Luther King Jr.'s speeches, because he was great at instilling emotion. He could stir passion, and as a young coach I was fascinated by people who could do that. I did the same thing with John F. Kennedy, studying his manner as well as his style. When I used to work at summer basketball camps I probably heard 150 different coaches come in and give speeches, everyone from low-key men like Dean Smith and Al McGuire to the more emotional and fiery Bobby Knight. I listened to the entertainers, who always managed to have their audiences eating out of the palm of their hand, and I also listened to those who were unable to captivate a crowd.

But from my research and my coaching, I have learned

that there are different kinds of communicating, depending on whom I am talking to. I've been giving motivational speeches to companies around the country for about ten years now, and when I am speaking to large groups what I am trying to do is create an excitement in the crowd. I have to be energetic, I have to have enthusiasm, and I have to be able to use my voice to reach everyone in the room. But again, what I am trying to do is stir a group's passion.

But speaking to one other person is totally different. This requires listening, never taking your eyes off that person, conveying the impression that this conversation is very important to you. It's talking in a calming, soothing tone. Here, you are not trying to stir a passion; you are trying to have a dialogue, to listen, to build trust, and to establish a relationship with the person.

When you are speaking on the phone it's the same thing. It's building a trust with someone far away. It's not about call waiting, leaving the conversation to go talk to someone else; call waiting is an incredible turnoff. Again, you must convey the impression that this is an important conversation to you, one that you are not treating cavalierly.

## SOMETIMES YOU HAVE TO IGNORE YOUR OWN AGENDA

I am always going into kids' homes on recruiting visits, trying to convince both the high school player and his family why he should choose Kentucky over the other schools.

I used to have my routine down: I would go in and make my presentation a performance, if you will. Often my assistant coaches would have laid the groundwork with the family, and I would come into the home for the big finish, like a salesman closing the deal.

I would talk about the strengths of the university, about how we play in front of 23,500 in Rupp Arena and play a national schedule and have the most loyal and rabid fans in the country. I would talk about the various academic programs, our academic support services, our weight-training facilities, and all the other things I could think of in hopes of convincing a high school player and his family that Kentucky was the best place for him. And I would do all of this with all the passion, enthusiasm, and persuasive skill I could muster.

Afterward, back in the car I would ask one of my assistant coaches, who was with me on the home visit, how he thought I had done.

"You were great, Coach," he would invariably say. "You covered everything. There's no way that we're not going to be one of his top choices, and we're probably going to get him."

Then we'd call the recruit the next day to follow up on the visit and learn that we weren't even in the player's top five schools. Essentially, we'd hear, "Thanks, but no thanks."

What had gone wrong? How had we failed?

And I would question myself: Hadn't I been enthusiastic enough? Hadn't I articulated our program well enough? What could I have done differently?

Eventually, I figured out that it had nothing to do with my performance. My failure had to do with my approach.

When I went out again on the home visits, I began to say very little. I would go in and essentially listen. What did the player want in a college and a college basketball program? What did the family want?

I let them do most of the talking and when I would go back to the car and ask my assistant how he thought the visit had gone he'd invariably say, "I don't know, Coach. You didn't mention the individual instruction. You didn't mention the academic support services. I don't feel real good about this one."

Then we'd do the follow up the next day and hear we were in the final two.

Why?

Because I had listened. I had allowed the other people to speak. I had made the other people believe their thoughts had value. I had started to build a relationship with people instead of giving them a performance. And I had learned a valuable lesson: It's not always what *we* say; often it's what we allow the *other* person to say. By listening, we gain trust and make other people feel more comfortable with us.

The correct ratio should be somewhere in the vicinity of four to one: Listen four times more than you speak. Use that as a basic rule of thumb, and you're heading in the right direction.

In addition to listening more often, one way to better communicate with people is to own up to your mistakes, the way I did with Bill Cartwright. By doing this, you not only disarm the other person but you instantly change the dynamics of the situation.

By admitting your mistakes, your inherent message is that you're trying to be conciliatory, that you really do want to correct the misunderstanding. Your doing this immediately takes the other person off the defensive and enables that person to be more willing to own up to his or her mistakes. This is what communication is all about. Because the goal is not to be right all the time. The goal is to win.

But let me stress what *winning* means.

We all know people who have to win every discussion, every argument. They are the ones forever talking both the loudest and the longest, as if every conversation had a winner and a loser. This approach is a losing one. Besides being ultimately obnoxious and tiresome, it sends the wrong message. It tells the person to whom you are talking that his or her opinion really doesn't count. It also tells that person your main intention in the discussion is to be right, not to arrive at any common ground.

If your goal in discussions is to always be right, then you will never be a good communicator. Winning arguments is not what it's about. Being right is not what this is all about. In life, winning is when both people can benefit, when you can leverage the personal connection that communication establishes to help both people achieve their goals.

## COMMUNICATE YOUR GOALS AND NEEDS

Never forget that so much of motivation is tied up in communication.

Let's use a rather mundane example.

Let's say I'm at home on the phone, and my three older children are in the room.

"Michael," I say to the oldest, "go out in the driveway and get the briefcase out of my car."

"Why me?" he says. "I'm busy. Why can't Chris get it?"

"Why can't Ricky get it?" says Chris.

"I got it last time," says Ricky.

All three of them feel as if they were being picked on. This happens in the workplace all the time. The boss tells someone to do something and his or her first reaction is "Why me? How come the boss is picking on me?" It's human nature.

So now all three kids have complained about being asked to go get my briefcase out of the car, and it's back to Michael again.

"Why me?" he asks.

"Because it's heavy, and you're the strongest," I tell him. "Plus, I need it quickly, and you're the oldest and can get it faster than the other two."

See the difference?

Now he feels differently about the task. Now he knows I selected him not as a form of punishment or by random luck of the draw but out of an awareness of his abilities. By taking a few seconds to explain to him the reason why he's being asked to do this, he now feels totally different about being asked to perform the task. I have spent the time to communicate with him, instead of just ordering him to do it.

You must communicate with people.

And the carrot always works better than the stick.

When I became the coach of the New York Knicks and first met Patrick Ewing—the best player on the team and the cornerstone of the franchise—my first words to him were how happy I was to have an opportunity to coach him. When we obtained Charles Oakley the following year in a trade—a player who had the reputation as someone who would either kill you or kill for you—my first words were of how much I loved him as a player. You are trying to build bridges to people, not set up moats.

People want to know *why* they are being asked to do something. It's not enough to say "because I told you so."

"I told you so" is an instant turnoff, maybe the biggest one there is, whether you're a parent, teacher, coach, employer, whatever. Certainly, there are times when it's unavoidable. But the small amount of time it takes to explain things usually pays big dividends.

Let's say one of my players is seeking my help in getting a job, but comes into my office with an earring and dressed in a way that you know is not going to impress an employer.

My first instinct might be to ask, "Are you serious? No one is going to hire you dressed like that. Go back to your room and change."

There's a better way, though.

All of us, once we get to a certain age, have convenient memories. We can't stand rap music, but forget that our parents couldn't stand rock 'n' roll. Just like their parents probably couldn't stand big band music. It's just the style of the times and to take it as a personal affront is short-sighted and foolish.

So I might say something like this to the particular player sitting in my office: "When I was your age I had long sideburns, and I could show you some pictures of me back then that would have you falling off the chair laughing. But as your adviser—your friend—I cannot let you go to an interview in the business world dressed like that, because they're just not going to hire you."

Now nine times out of ten this young man will listen.

Why?

Because he wants to be successful too.

The point is you're not telling him you disapprove of his lifestyle. You're telling him that the way he's dressed will not help him succeed in finding a job. On the surface it might not seem like that big a difference. But it's major.

Take this past season, for example.

The problem I had going in was that I had too many good players. Too many who deserved to play.

Doesn't sound like a bad problem, right?

Wrong.

In sports, very often having too many good players is just as much a negative as having too few. Having too many players often creates jealousies and dissension, cancers that eat at the heart of any group. So I knew that if we didn't find a way to solve this problem as a team, we definitely were not going to be in any position to win a national championship. I wondered what to do about it. Then one day in the fall I met with the team and told them about my problem.

I said, "Here is the problem I have as a coach, and you are either all going to help me solve it or I'm going to solve it myself autocratically. Which one is it going to be?"

The point is I gave them a chance to be part of the solution. I made them aware of the problem right in the beginning and gave them a big stake in the potential solution of it. This reinforced to those players who didn't figure to see a lot of playing time that it wasn't because I didn't value them as players. It also instantly brought them all closer together as a team. They understood they were all being asked to sacrifice some of their individual goals in the name of the collective good; and that if we all somehow found a way to solve this problem, they had a chance to become part of basketball history, to become part of something special. Which is what ended up happening. The fact that every one of our players understood the goal we had to accomplish resulted in the 1996 NCAA Championship.

## CONFRONT PROBLEMS IMMEDIATELY

Problems don't go away by themselves.

It's human nature to want to have problems disappear by themselves, to believe that time really does heal all wounds. It doesn't. If you let problems fester they usually only get worse.

Yes, sometimes it makes sense to sleep on a problem and not react spontaneously, or out of emotion or anger. But once you've calmed down, it's best to deal with people right away to talk things out. Not in an in-your-face confrontational way. But by listening and trying to communicate.

Let's say you're having trouble with your boss and you don't think your boss likes you.

What do you do about it?

What many people do is ignore it and hope it goes away. Or else they complain to everyone around them that their boss doesn't like them. Either way, it's the wrong approach, one that can only lead to future unhappiness

The only way to truly address the situation is by connecting with individuals.

You communicate with them.

You ask these people for a few minutes of their time and then simply ask them if they have a problem with you. Not in a hostile manner. Not by trying to put them on the defensive. Not to fight with them. But by saying that you sense there's a problem, it's got you concerned, and you'd like to try to straighten it out.

So many times you will find that (1) you've overreacted and the person really doesn't have any negative feelings about you or (2) the problem is a result of a misunderstanding, something that automatically will get better as soon as you clear things up.

The point is that you've given the problem a forum in which it can be resolved. This is always better than letting it hang over your head where all it does is create anxiety, discontent, and the potential to magnify. For there's nothing that pollutes the workplace more than rumors and third-hand gossip from disgruntled employees who can't be adults about their work problems.

These are poisons and must be neutralized whenever possible. They suck the joy out of the workplace, turning it into a grim, oppressive place. They cause stress. They make us doubt both ourselves and the people around us. If you don't try to communicate to resolve them you are allowing them to fester.

Maybe you will find out that your boss does have a problem with you, whether it's your performance, work ethic, attitude, whatever. If so, at least you have identified what the specific problem is and can now possibly take steps to correct it. If nothing else, your bringing it to the boss's attention tells him or her that this is a concern of yours, something you want to rectify. This makes you look like a committed person and lets your boss know that your job is important to you.

And if you find out that this person does have a problem with you, something that can't be resolved?

At least you now know, and can then act accordingly. Because sometimes problems arise in the workplace that are irresolvable, whether they're personality conflicts or something else. Then you have a choice: Depending on your economic situation, you can leave or start looking to change jobs or possibly rethink your career choices.

Or else you can try to find ways to make the best of unfortunate circumstances, for the simple reason that your personal situation doesn't allow you to leave. It doesn't make much sense to walk across the street to get out of the rain, if across the street is just more rain.

Either way, you have taken action. You have stopped living in the past and have done something to prepare for the future. You have exerted some control over the situation, rather than being controlled by it. You have done that by communicating.

## REINFORCE GOOD PERFORMANCES

Minutes after we won the national championship at the Brendan Byrne Arena in the Meadowlands and had come back into the locker room I sensed that Antoine Walker, our star sophomore, was not as happy as he should have been. Although we had won, he had not had one of his better games, and I could sense that was bothering him.

Now Antoine is a great talent, but he had come to Kentucky from Chicago as a great high school player who was selfish with the ball, the kind of player who never met a shot he didn't like. That never bothered me, because a lot of high school stars are selfish, and Antoine had been one of the most highly recruited high school players in the country. I recruited him because he was a great competitor, and because his first choice was to come to Kentucky.

My task as a motivator then was to make him more team oriented, while not putting a blanket on either his talent or his competitiveness.

It's a delicate balance. You need to have the player think "team" first and realize that the group's success is more important than his own, but you also don't want him to lose his individual uniqueness as a player. As a coach, it's a little like walking on a tightrope.

So when Antoine began using his passing skills and began playing less selfishly, I publicly pointed this out. Wherever I had the chance, I would tell people that Antoine's willingness to alter his own game was what was making us a great team.

At the large press conference in the Meadowlands the day before the Final Four began—with Antoine there as one of the players with me—I said that at no time in my four years in the NBA (two as head coach of the Knicks and two as an assistant) was how many points a college player scored ever discussed when we were assessing pro potential and that what was discussed was how much a particular player helped his team win.

Again, this was another message to Antoine that being

unselfish and placing the success of the team above his own aspirations would benefit him in the long run.

With Antoine, as with all my players and with all people you are trying to lead, you must constantly stress to everyone that when the group does well everyone benefits. When the sea rises, all the boats rise with it. It's true in sports. It's true in business. It's true in life.

And when you're asking people to subordinate some of their individual goals for the sake of the group, you must let them know you are aware of their sacrifice.

You must constantly thank them for it. Praising people in front of their peers is a very positive motivational tool.

At each of the press conferences in the NCAA tournament I made it a point not only to praise our team's selflessness, but Antoine's in particular. Not only as a reinforcement tool, but to tell both him and his teammates that I truly appreciated what he was doing.

So when I saw in the locker room that Antoine wasn't as happy as he should have been, I quickly took him into the bathroom, hugged him, and told him the truth: I thanked him for giving me the best moment of my basketball life. Thanked him for his unselfishness and for being such an important part of our team. Made him aware that without him we wouldn't have won the national championship. He instantly brightened and was fine after that.

That's what you have to do if you are the leader of a group, whether it's a boss, a teacher, a parent, a coach. You must reinforce good performances.

You also must define the role of each person.

As people gain more experience and wisdom, as they mature and are nurtured through the system, their roles will definitely change and become more important. People have to know this, to realize that although their role may be relatively minor now, it doesn't always have to be that way. More important, they have to know that their work effort and their performance determines how quickly their role changes.

But as I talked about in Step 1, people must be aware they're involved in something significant. Remember, it's not enough just to be part of a group anymore. Those days are over. To pretend that people automatically know their value only brings on low morale and frustration in the work environment. Not only do people want to feel that what they're doing is important, they want to know that their efforts are appreciated.

People must also be made to understand that there will be a tangible reward if the group is successful. It might be more money. It might be added respect from their peers. It might be external praise. But it will be something. Just as it was constantly stressed to Antoine Walker that he would benefit personally if the team did well, people must know that they will benefit if their leader does well and vice versa. It's the essence of any great organization.

## DON'T BURN BRIDGES

The art of listening is looking at someone when he or she speaks to you, not over his or her shoulder at who else might be in the room.

It's hearing what the person is saying to you instead of thinking about what you're going to say next.

It's making eye contact, which not only is courteous but gives the person with whom you're speaking the sense that you truly care what he or she is saying to you. Making eye contact develops trust.

It's being attentive, creating the impression that this conversation is important to you, that you value it. And you can't let shyness be an excuse. You must look people in the eye and pay attention. It is at the core of the art of listening.

At a basic level, this is merely being courteous, treating people the way we would like to be treated.

It's also just smart.

None of us knows what lies down the road. We don't know what's going to happen to the people we are meeting now.

Who knows? Someday those people you're virtually dismissing could be in a position to help you in business. What impression are you making on them? You must remember that first impressions can be very powerful. You must remember that we are all in the business of trying to create the best impression possible and we never know who is watching us, assessing us.

Once I was talking to a sports writer I knew who happened to be standing with someone else. I completely ignored the other person, almost to the point of being rude. Later, I learned that person was the sports editor of one of the biggest newspapers in the country.

I don't know exactly what impression that person got of me, but I know it wasn't good. Why should it have been? I learned a lesson that day, one that's stayed with me.

This past summer at the PGA championship in Louisville there was a story about how Kevin Costner was asked by a woman for his autograph.

Costner refused, essentially telling the woman, "I'm not your pen pal."

Well, she went on WHAS, a large radio station in Louisville, and told the story. Now I don't know Kevin Costner, but

I have several friends who do, and they all like him and say he's down to earth, without pretense.

But he slipped that day. In his defense, maybe the woman caught him at a bad moment. But the point is that one comment, later broadcast over a radio station with a large signal, was the kind of publicity Kevin Costner clearly doesn't want or need. All because of one remark. And the irony is that it probably took as much energy for him to say no as it would have to sign the autograph.

So there's a lesson for you in this little story.

Use your energy in a positive way.

Try to create allies, not enemies.

One of the most difficult parts of my job is dealing with the media and realizing that eventually someone is going to write something about me that I don't think is fair. There are two ways to handle this: I can turn the other cheek, say that what that person writes is her opinion and she's entitled to it no matter how unfair I think it might be, then move on. Or else I can pick up the phone and deal with that person.

As a young coach I used to say "The hell with it" when someone wrote something about me that I thought was not only wrong but unfair. I didn't think it was important to spend time clearing things up.

Now, at age forty-four, I've learned that that's not always the best way to deal with it. Maybe there's some sense of truth to what the writer said. Maybe it's the result of some sort of misunderstanding or misinterpretation.

But the only way to find out is to communicate with that person. Otherwise, it all gets complicated. You see so much of that: He said this, she said that, then he said something else. Around and around it goes; and where it ends, nobody knows. Only that it's never good.

The way to correct this?

Pick up the phone.

Communicate.

It may not get anything resolved, but by trying to resolve the problem, you begin to turn a negative into a positive. You open the door for reconciliation and perhaps a better opportunity in the future.

## Key Points for Step 5

Just like any other habit, keep working on making yourself a great communicator.

△

And communicating is less about speaking than about listening.

△

Avoid having to be right all the time.

△

The goal is to connect, not defeat.

△

Communicate your goals and needs to other people. People won't respond to "because I told you so." They need to know they have an important role in the process. Confront problems immediately, head-on. Problems don't disappear in a puff of smoke, nor do they go away if you avoid them. In fact, they usually only get worse.

△

How you relate to people in the workplace—both those above you and those below you—is vital, because you never know who might one day be your boss.

## REAL PASSION MAKES
## COMMUNICATION EASY

I heard Rick Pitino speak on several occasions—once when he gave a speech to our company and a couple of times when he allowed me in the locker room at University of Kentucky games.

What really struck me the most was the level of focus Rick and his staff put into preparing the players for the game. It was amazing. As I listened to him, I kept saying, "God, can you do this in business?"

What quickly became clear to me was the true depth of his passion to succeed. He is such a forceful, powerful speaker that it's easy to get caught up in what he's saying. And you can see that his passion is real. That's very evident. I know that all of my employees who heard him speak were as impressed with him as I was.

At about the same time I heard Rick speak, our company was in the process of going public. The take-away I got from listening to him—from seeing his passion—was not to be embarrassed by having my own passion for my own business I had always had the passion, but I had been somewhat reluctant to show it. After seeing Rick, I changed. No longer am I reluctant to show my passion, whether it's to my employees, or to our investors.

In terms of motivation, and of being a great motivator, I don't think there's a better one than Rick Pitino.

**Chris Sullivan**
CHAIRMAN AND CEO, OUTBACK STEAKHOUSES, INC.

# 6 LEARN FROM ROLE MODELS

I learned at a young age that you could learn a lot from the experiences of people around you, lessons that you can make part of your own arsenal.

I went to college in the early 1970s, a time of great racial tension at the University of Massachusetts. The man who had first recruited me to UMass was a black man named Ray Wilson, who once had been Julius Erving's high school coach and had seen me play a high school game in the Long Island Coliseum. We took an instant liking to each other, to the point that after talking to him for just fifteen minutes I knew I wanted to go to UMass.

But that's not the biggest gift Ray Wilson gave me.

He taught me my first big lesson on how to trust people.

Ray broke down all the racial barriers because he never dealt with people in terms of black and white. Race was never a label to him, like it was to so many other people. He transcended color in the way he dealt with everyone; and despite the tendencies of most around him, made no distinctions based on race. He made it impossible to have prejudices, taught me it didn't matter whether you were black or white, city or suburban, we were all people. He was always himself and showed me the value of sticking to your guns even when you're going against the grain.

He also taught me the importance of listening. I was an emotional kid; and he would often give me the chance to rant and rave, the chance to vent, and then he would simply state his opinion very matter-of-factly. He befriended me at a very vulnerable time for me, and always was a very calming influence. He would watch my highly charged youthful performance for a while, then he'd say, "Are you listening to yourself, Rick? Are you listening to yourself?"

He became a very large role model in my life. To this day, whenever I talk about the ability to listen in communicating with people—like I talked about in Step 5—I am paying a tribute to Ray Wilson and his influence on me.

But there is a point here that transcends the specifics of what Ray Wilson gave me.

Once you've established your work ethic, once you've demonstrated that you're willing to arrive early, stay late, and put in the effort it's going to take to be successful, you are on your way to becoming a motivated person. Now, you must become equally committed to doing things the correct way. Remember, perfect *practice* makes perfect.

How do you find the right way?

You must remember that many people have made the journey before you. Some of them enjoyed success; some of them experienced failure. All of them can teach you something. Role models can enable you to learn from experience you haven't had yet, or may never have.

But what are role models, and how can we use them?

Understand, we all model those around us, even if we don't know we're doing it. Newborn animals mimic behavior from their mothers. Little children take on habits of their parents. Later they learn from what they see around them, whether it's their peers, teachers, or what they see in movies or on television. It's the way we come of age.

You see this in sports all the time. Kids go out to the playground and model what they saw the great players do on television the night before. They copy those great moves and try to incorporate them into their own games. Children model teenagers—everything from tastes in clothes to language. Adults look in magazines to see what to wear, what to put in their homes, what car to drive. Modeling is how we learn in life.

Identifying role models, though, is a little more complicated. In theory, role models are the people we look up to, the ones we want to emulate. But if they really are to help us, we need to define what role models are.

Role models are not necessarily people you admire or people you are fans of. You may like Barbra Streisand's music, but that doesn't mean she should be your role model. You may like Tom Cruise in the movies, but that doesn't necessarily mean he has anything to teach you that's going to help you work better. That's a mistake many people make. They confuse a celebrity with a role model. Role models are not *Billboard*'s Top 10 musicians. They're not necessarily the people you had hanging on your bedroom walls when you were a kid. These are the people who entertain you.

Role models are people you can emulate, people you can learn things from. And you'll find them everywhere, from the person sitting next to you at work to someone in your family. A role model is anyone who has anything to teach you on your journey to success.

## WHO ARE USEFUL ROLE MODELS?

First you have to do research. You have to know your subject. And you are not going to be like a teenager doing some form of "The Dating Game." You don't want to marry these people or have dates with them or know their favorite colors or join their fan clubs. You are not trying to *be* them. It's like the person who buys a Brioni suit because he wants to be like Pierce Brosnan. Well, he's going to end up with a beautiful suit, one that's finely crafted and well made. But he's not going to be Pierce Brosnan. He's just going to be the same guy in a better suit. So you have to understand what you're trying to get from people. What you are trying to do is identify those qualities you admire, see where they come from.

Someone in a television commercial might say, "I want to be like Mike," in homage to Michael Jordan, but that's not what we're talking about. Modeling is a way of saying that we respect and admire the abilities of certain people, qualities that we want to make ours.

Is this possible?

Yes.

Again, you're not marrying a role model. You're not bringing him or her into your family. You're trying to learn something about that person's gifts and talents, and you're trying to incorporate them into your own behavior. You're not interested in his or her public persona, the face this person shows to the world. You're interested in the process, the traits that allowed him or her to be successful in the first place.

So you shouldn't be interested in people who have been successful because they've been lucky, like people who have been born into great wealth or married into it. Leave that to the supermarket tabloids. You should be looking for the people who have become successful through their own achievements and hard work.

Role models don't have to be celebrities. In fact, it's probably better if they're not. I hope that your role models are people you know, people whom you look up to daily for specific traits, not just because you admire their talents. These are the ones who can provide constant inspiration and wisdom as you work toward your goals.

You should also look at role models who are at the same stage you are so that you can better measure yourself against what they're doing. For instance, who are the people in your age group who are more successful than you and why? If you are a student, ask yourself why your roommate is getting better grades than you are. If you are a salesman, why is your coworker selling more? What tricks is she using that you aren't? Is her work ethic better? More important, what can you learn from her?

These people have things to teach you.

Some people become role models for a very specific time and for a very specific purpose. As a child I read the story of Helen Keller, who overcame her disabilities, learning to read, write, and speak and becoming a noted author, speaker, and advocate for the handicapped. I remember how moved I was at the time reading about her life, how inspiring it was. Knowing her story has to make you think you could move mountains in your own life.

Is she one of my role models today?

Not really.

But there's no question that her story had an impact on me when I read it. Just as I've remembered the books I've read on Abraham Lincoln, who overcame a difficult childhood, many political defeats, the death of two sons, a nervous breakdown, deep depression, loneliness, and constant public criticism to become arguably the greatest president in U.S. history.

It's impossible to read about Lincoln and not be moved both by his incredible perseverance and by his sense of moral purpose. It's impossible to read about Lincoln and not become instantly aware that his story has lessons for everyone.

As does the story of Jackie Robinson, who broke the color barrier in major league baseball, and might have been the most disciplined athlete ever. He was extremely gifted athletically, but he also was cantankerous, biting, and hot tempered. Yet, before he was allowed to sign with the Brooklyn Dodgers, he swore to Branch Rickey that he would not respond to taunts, racial slurs, beanings, and threats for the first two years of his career. His play on the field, along with his ability to control his temper and maintain a state of grace, won fans over and made it easier for other blacks to follow.

Are they my role models?

Certainly they are in a general sense, simply for the lessons they have for all of us and their ability to inspire us. That's why I enjoy reading books about great figures in history. Not only are their personal journeys so incredible, but I always come away from such books believing in the power of the human spirit, the feeling that virtually anything is possible if we truly can become as dedicated and focused as these people were. I come away both educated and uplifted.

But our role models don't have to be great figures from history. Far from it. However, if they are, we are looking for the specific traits that made them successful, not the panoramic scope of their lives. How hard did they work? What did they have to overcome? How much persistence did they show? How did they manage to overcome all the adversity they faced, what was it about them as people that made them so successful?

These are the things you should be constantly seeking.

It's the answers to these questions that have the potential

to really help us. For there is a tendency to think that people who went on to accomplish extraordinary things are somehow so very different from us. The sense that these great things just sort of happened to these people, as if by fate or divine intervention.

Yet the more you examine their lives the more you become aware that this is simply not true. These people weren't just lucky. Many of them didn't have any more physical or mental gifts than you have. These people accomplished extraordinary things because they had extraordinary discipline. They refused to be denied in the pursuit of their dreams. They refused to be thwarted by failure and used those failures as springboards to later success. They were relentless in pursuit of their goals. That is the message their lives tell you. It is up to you to hear it.

Yet my role models can change by the month. I am always studying people, studying what works and what doesn't, always looking for ways to make myself and my team more successful. There is no overestimating the value of this. Because it's very simple: If we are not getting better, we are getting worse. There's no staying the same. So I am constantly looking for new role models who might teach me new lessons.

Recently, I read an article in *Sky* magazine about Jerry Rice, the great wide receiver for the San Francisco 49ers. It was about his great work ethic, how even at this stage of his career, after all his success and all his rewards, he has a workout routine that no one can keep up with.

The quickie résumé on Rice is this: He grew up in rural Mississippi and did not even play Division I football, going instead to a small Division II school called Mississippi Valley State. Though he was drafted in the first round by the 49ers, there were plenty of doubters. Some thought he was too slow to ever really be an effective NFL wide receiver. Some felt he hadn't played against strong enough competition in college. But Jerry Rice has gone on to become perhaps the greatest wide receiver in the history of professional football, setting records in career yardage and touchdowns.

That's the condensed version.

And how has he done this?

Has he done it exclusively by great natural ability? Has he done it by being more athletically gifted than others? Has he done it by simply wishing it? No. He has done it by endless hours of hard work, a regimen he was introduced to by one of his former 49er teammates, running back Roger Craig.

Consider this typical off-season workout, one that Rice does religiously:

After a strenuous warm-up of stretching, he starts off with what he calls "stop and go's," which consist of running five yards up the field and back, then forty yards up the field and back. He does this seven times, rests briefly, then does it seven more times. Then he does something called "triangle cones," which consist of accelerating quickly on an angle to a cone, then changing direction and heading toward another cone. He does three sets of these, then three more.

This is followed by running forty yards down the sideline carrying the ball. He does six sets of these with no rest between sets. Then he sprints twenty yards down the field, makes a fake, and catches a thrown ball. This is done over and over until exhaustion.

Then he goes and lifts weights: multiple sets of bench presses, seated bench presses on machines, incline bench presses, and dumbbell curls with increasing weights and lower reps per set, maxing out with a two-rep power lift. This is all done with quick rotation between stations, with little rest between exercises.

Now remember that this is Jerry Rice, arguably the greatest wide receiver in the history of professional football. This is someone who already has achieved virtually everything there is to achieve in his profession. Yet each day in the off-season he still puts himself through this type of grueling workout.

Is it any wonder that Rice says he hasn't lost a step to age, has never been injured, and feels he can play as long as he wants to?

"See, lots of guys say they want to be the best," Rice told *Sky* magazine, "but they're not willing to do the little things. I'm willing to make the sacrifices, to do the work. I mean, I dare anyone to come out and hang with me. Full out, no holding back. Seriously, there's not many out there with my endurance. Or my desire."

So Jerry Rice has become one of my new role models. Again, I am not marrying Jerry Rice. I know I'll probably never meet him. Nor is that important. But what is important is that I take the essence of what makes him successful and incorporate that into my philosophy.

But I am going to make sure every one of my players reads that *Sky* magazine article and realizes the price Jerry Rice pays to be as great as he is. I will try to learn from him, use him as a model for how hard I want my players to work.

I do this all the time with my players. I'm always giving them things to read about someone's work ethic or an athlete's competitiveness, something I think my players can use. It helps, obviously, if those people are celebrities because there's instant identification. But that's not the most important thing. I am looking for the specific things that make those people successful, almost as if I could break it down into little parts and put them under a microscope, so that my players could both see these things and learn something from them.

That's the point: to learn and to understand what got them there.

Otherwise, I would have little interest in Jerry Rice's workout schedule, other than a certain curiosity. But by using his workout schedule as both an educational and a motivational tool for my players, I have made that article on Jerry Rice work for me.

There are reasons why when a Pat Riley becomes the coach of the Miami Heat everyone knows that team is going to get appreciably better, but when other coaches get jobs there is not that same attitude. There are reasons why when Peter Ueberroth became the head of the 1984 Olympics everyone knew it was going to be a success. There are reasons why David Stern turned the NBA into a textbook example of marketing genius, a blueprint for every CEO in the country. These are the people we want to study and emulate.

And the key word is *study*. Not admire. Study.

The other person I'm studying now is Jimmy Johnson, the new coach of the Miami Dolphins, someone who has a reputation of taking football programs and immediately making them better. How does he do it? What are his beliefs? What are his methods? Are they the same as mine or different?

If he does some things differently do I want to use them? If he does some things the same way, that's something I can use as reinforcement.

And I don't care about Jimmy Johnson's personal life. I don't care whether people like him. I don't care what he does in his private life. I am simply interested in those things that make him a successful football coach and if I can use any of them. Everything else is irrelevant.

You also can't be afraid to adapt someone else's ideas and make them your own. But don't just copy them. Tinker with them. Build on them. Make them fit your personality. That's where the creativity comes in. Always ask yourself, "How is this going to fit into my game plan?"

It's like the concept of a "model home." You know the ones. They're the first ones built in a new development. Everything is done just right. All the best amenities. All the best features. But that's not necessarily how your house is going to look. It's just the model. You look at it, decide what works for you and what doesn't. It's the same with role models. Take what works for you. Leave the rest.

You always must be looking to reinforce your own beliefs through someone else. You always should be putting your own methods under a microscope. You always must be adapting what you're doing, always trying to make it better. Because the times keep changing, and you must change with them.

The way I coached when I was at Boston University back in the 1970s wouldn't work today. I have had to make adjustments in almost every aspect of my coaching strategy. If you don't change, you'll get passed by. And one of the ways you can change is by always looking for role models and trying to assimilate what they do into your own repertoire.

Now understand that when you're looking for models of action, you're not looking for gimmicks.

That's the trouble today. People want shortcuts, whether it's the easiest way to have better abs or the quickest way to have a better physique or whatever the goal of the moment is. People are trying to work fewer hours and four-day weeks, and every day there seems to be more hollow strategies, more trendy things, more approaches designed to make life easier. People are looking to work less and be rewarded more.

But you must never forget that you must *deserve* victory, never forget that when it comes to being successful there are no shortcuts. It takes work, and lots of it. It goes back to that discipline I talked about in the introduction. It goes back to having that organized plan of attack. It all goes back to your building blocks. You can't forget that even as there are things around you that supposedly make your days easier—whether it's fax machines, computers, cellular phones, etc.—they are not substitutes for a work ethic second to none.

So when you go looking for role models you are not looking for people who do things the easy way. You're not looking for people who take shortcuts. You're not looking for people who hit the lottery or did something lucky. Luck is for bingo halls, work is for life. You're looking for people who have traits you admire. You are looking for those qualities that you want to make part of your own arsenal of winning behavior. You are looking for people who inspire you to seek new heights.

## HOW DO YOU LEARN FROM THEM?

While I was a student at UMass I worked a station at the Five Star summer basketball camp in Honesdale, Pennsylvania—a station being a place where a player works on a specific skill—and coached a team in both the younger and older divisions. I was the youngest person ever to do so.

It was a great introduction to the whole process; but more important, I was able to learn from the established college coaches who were also working the camp. They would give lectures about the intricacies of coaching strategy and specific things individual players can do to make themselves better, and I would study them carefully. What worked? What didn't? How did they hold the attention of the audience?

Three of my first models were Hubie Brown, who later became the coach of the Atlanta Hawks and New York Knicks in the NBA; Chuck Daly, who coached the Detroit Pistons to two world championships; and Jimmy Lynam, now the coach of Washington in the NBA. From Hubie I learned the importance of using my voice to take control of a group, to command respect. From Daly I learned how to get players to watch and listen by the way I carried myself. And from Lynam I learned the importance of being able to do the drills myself, of impressing kids with my own basketball ability. When I became a coach and did a lot of lectures on shooting at camps I always was my own demonstrator, shooting the ball and making shots as I talked.

I wasn't trying to copy any one of them exactly, but I took something away from all my predecessors and made it a part of my repertoire.

I first started reading about Vince Lombardi when I was in college. I saw one of those "NFL Flashback" programs about the glory days of the Green Bay Packers; then I watched a movie about Lombardi with Ernest Borgnine and became obsessed with how he conducted himself.

Lombardi was one of the greatest football coaches in history, the man who led the Green Bay Packers to the top of the NFL in the 1960s. He not only understood the power of motivation but also had the ability to translate it to the players he coached. He was a master at developing championship teams, and his methods were many—an iron will, an inexhaustible belief in himself and his system, the uncanny knack for getting average players to perform far beyond their talent level. But none of his skills was greater than his ability to turn a group of disparate individuals into a cohesive unit that was willing to lay everything on the line for the good of the team.

"Individual commitment to a group effort," Lombardi said. "That's what makes a team work, a company work, a society work, a civilization work."

153

I remember the first time I saw the quote. I was mesmerized.

I started reading everything I could get my hands on about Lombardi. I was fascinated with him: the way he spoke, the way he demanded things. I started adopting many of the principles he taught. The mixture of love and discipline. The development of character. That was the whole thing: character as an attitude.

When I first got into coaching I quickly discovered my success was going to be tied directly to how much my players achieved, and I could help them to do that by instituting some of the things I already had learned from older coaches, whether it was the coaches I once had studied at Five Star, or my readings about Vince Lombardi.

That's an example of role modeling at its best. I wasn't trying to be like Hubie Brown, Chuck Daly, or Jimmy Lynam. I wasn't trying to be like Vince Lombardi. I was trying to be an amalgamation of all of them, specifically of those qualities in each person that I not only identified with but thought I could incorporate into my own coaching style.

I often get young coaches who tell me that I'm their role model, that they want to be like me, and I am flattered. But I think that many of them are not stating it correctly. What they should be saying is, "I want to emulate your coaching philosophy, your style of play, how hard your players work." That would be beneficial. Not to try to be me, because they don't really know me, but to copy certain behaviors to import into their own methods.

My two years as a Knicks assistant also helped my growth considerably, as I learned from the incredible role models around me. Hubie Brown was a master at preparation, for leaving no stone unturned. He would give the Knicks players pages of scouting reports, even though he knew they would never be able to retain it all, his theory being that even if they retained only 30 percent of what he gave them it was better than nothing. Today, I try to keep my players just as prepared, having learned the benefits of this directly from Hubie and its effect on the team.

I also learned in those two years that my way of doing things is not the only way. Other people can be right even if they don't do things the way I do them. Professional coaching also reinforces the fact that you, as the coach, are part of a team, much more so than in college sports when the coach's word is the absolute word. You learn that sometimes you have to stifle your own ego and do what's best for the team. But you must also find a way for everyone to pull for each other.

Later, my exploration led to other great motivators, everything from *The Power of Positive Thinking* to *The One Minute Manager* to Anthony Robbins to Pat Riley, even to characters in novels who overcame adversity to do heroic things. I have taken things from all of them, whether it's learning new methods for motivating people, or simply a reaffirmation of things I already believed. But it's more than just what I've learned from books and other motivational speakers. Every person I meet I try to steal from. When I hear someone say something I like, I borrow it, make it mine.

I've always done this. It's just always made sense to me. Learn from others. Learn from people who have made the journey before you. Learn from their wisdom.

If we're all going through life trying to be smarter, trying to do things better and more efficiently, than it only makes sense to learn everything we can from the people around us. Such a person can be anyone. The key is to focus in on the one thing that person has that you want to emulate.

So many people have things to teach you, if you are receptive to it. It may be your boss; it may be your golf buddy;

it may even be your mother. So people can be used as re-sources, if you only see them in that context. Again, you're not looking to become that person. You're not looking to look like that person, or wear the same clothes, or have the same mannerisms. You're trying to identify the things about that person that make him or her successful, and use them for yourself. Maybe it's your next-door neighbor who is up jogging his second mile as you are stooping over for your morning paper. Maybe it's your co-worker who works an hour later than you do everyday—and she's the one who just got a promotion. There is something we can learn from each of them.

I got a call from a colleague in the coaching field, Bernie Bickerstaff, the general manager of the Denver Nuggets in the NBA. He had traded for Mark Jackson—whom I talked about earlier in the book—and he wanted to know how I was successful in getting Mark to play so well when I coached him with the New York Knicks. This is modeling. Bernie is using me as part of his research on Mark, will undoubtedly take what I say, talk to others who know Mark, then incorporate all of his research into his own personality and his own methods.

That's smart.

That's an example of the type of research you should do.

## LEARN WHAT NOT TO DO

Learning what not to do is sometimes more important than learning what to do.

Why keep repeating the mistakes of the past?

That's a lesson I learned from my father. He was always telling me not to make the mistakes he did. "Why duplicate mistakes?" he would say. "Why keep doing the same dumb thing over and over?" He taught me that although it was human to make mistakes, it was stupid to keep repeating the same mistakes, a lesson I carry with me to this day.

One of the first things I did when I became the head coach at Boston University when I was just twenty-five was to hire two assistant coaches who were both significantly older than I, one by eighteen years, one by more than twenty years. I did the same thing when I became coach of the New York Knicks, relying on Dick McGuire and Fuzzy Levane, two men who had been in the organization for decades. As a young coach I had a feeling for the game and an idea of what to do; but by surrounding myself with so much wisdom, I gave myself every advantage. Remember: People with a lot of experience can tell you what not to do and often that's as important as knowing what to do.

We all have failings, of course. So what I've tried to do as a coach is to take what is good from people I've worked for and learn from the things that are not so good. When I was an assistant at Syracuse, for instance, I saw that Jim Boeheim was easy on his players. Don't misunderstand. Jim Boeheim is an excellent coach who has been unbelievably successful. He is a bright, articulate man, and we are very friendly. But we are total opposites. It is his nature to be easy on his players. That works for him; it doesn't work for me.

When I got to Boston University and had my own head coaching job, I knew I was going to be tougher on my players than Jim had been on his at Syracuse. It was my personality to play hard and to be competitive, and I wanted my players to reflect my personality on the court. At Boston University I pushed my players to just about the absolute level of human endurance. And I learned two things: There are few limitations to what the human mind and body can do, and you can be very tough on players as long as they know you care about them. The key is not getting people to work hard. The key is to get them *to like* working hard.

I also discovered that there were different ways to motivate people, for everyone wasn't the same or had the same needs or aspirations, and it was up to me as the motivator to find out what those things were.

But as a young coach then, and like so many young people, I was operating more on instinct than wisdom. I knew we were working hard and giving great effort, but I didn't know why we were winning. And by age twenty-five I was disciplined, organized, good at setting goals, and diligent about doing my homework; and I knew I was learning a lot about how to coach. I didn't really understand the methods of my own success, but I would still keep learning.

By my fifth year at Boston University I was not as tough on my players as I had been my first year. Partly it was just a matter of my own maturity; partly it was because my players had been internalizing the work ethic and so I didn't have to ride them quite as hard.

The other thing I learned was not to be so negative. Threats and screaming can motivate people in the short run, but after a while your players get beaten down emotionally and before you know it they're just waiting for the season to end.

That's when I thought of Jim Boeheim again. He may have been too easy on his players for my taste, but he always supported his kids. They, in turn, always loved to play for him. And that can be as important an ingredient in success as any other.

So Jim Boeheim taught me twice: first, when he taught me how *not* to handle my players; and later, when I saw the real value in his method. I learned how to incorporate the methods I could use into my own coaching philosophy. If you think about some of the experts who've helped you, you'll probably reach the same conclusion I have. Some of their lessons are obvious and immediate. But other lessons may take half a lifetime to discover. They were right there in front of you all along, of course; but you just weren't ready for them.

When you do finally learn these subtler lessons, you're well on your way to understanding how to choose the right way to do just about anything. And when you've found that kind of wisdom, you've done more than choose success. You've begun to live it.

## Key Points for Step 6

Learning from others can often help you make up for your own lack of experience. This is a valuable lesson. People all around you have things to teach you, and you must be receptive to them. You must take advantage of people who have made the journey ahead of you.

△

It's important to pick the right role models. You're not looking for people who entertain you or people who make you feel good. You're looking for people who can help you.

△

Role models are not simply people you like and admire. The key is to look for traits in people that can help you be more successful. You're not looking to join a fan club. You're looking for specific traits other people have that you can incorporate into your own repertoire.

△

Take advantage of the fact that you can learn from the mistakes of others. You can learn different approaches to overcoming challenges and select which ones work for you and which ones don't. Which ones fit your personality and which ones don't. Learning what not to do is often as important as learning what to do.

# EXCITEMENT IS
# CONTAGIOUS

When I first read in the papers that Rick Pitino was thinking of hiring a female for his coaching staff I thought he was being a very courageous, very innovative individual, because no major men's basketball program had ever had a woman assistant coach before.

But at the time, I certainly didn't associate myself with what he was trying to do. I certainly knew who he was, and my husband—fiancé at the time—had attended several of Rick's basketball camps, but I had never thought about coaching at Kentucky.

I was an assistant coach on the women's team at the University of Georgia at the time, so when I got a call from one of Rick's assistants asking me if I had any interest in the job, I couldn't believe it. Naturally, I said I would consider it. A day or so later Rick called. We talked about the job, what my duties would be and all; and a few days later he offered me the job.

I've always appreciated what he did, not only for what he did for me, but because it took a lot of courage on his part to hire a female assistant. It was a first, and anytime there's a first there's going to be some resistance. But Rick never cared about that. One of the first things I learned about him is that he doesn't let public opinion influence his decision making.

To me, that's the mark of a real leader. Someone who has the courage to adhere to his own beliefs rather than do what is safe or expected. In the five or six years I've been around Rick, I've seen him do the right thing, even if it wasn't the most popular thing at the time.

Rick also has the unique ability to make players think they are better than they are. To make them perform above their capabilities. I think it's a direct result of the fact that he believes so strongly in himself and his system that there's just no way he's going to fail.

He's also a master at getting players to play with a lot of heart and passion. If you have talent—but no heart or passion—you're just not going to be successful, no matter what you're are doing. But on the flip side, if you have minimal talent but a lot of heart, you have a chance to do very well. That's what happened with his first couple of teams at Kentucky. He had guys with limited athletic ability, but they had enough heart and desire and love of the game that it enabled them to overachieve.

There's just such a positive aura around Rick. He does not for a second think he's going to fail, and he's so committed to what he's doing. When you see someone with that much love for what he's doing, you can't help but feel the same level of excitement.

Now that I've become a head coach myself, the one thing I want to do is match him when it comes to working hard. He is an unbelievably tireless worker. I think that those are the three key things I learned from him: hard work, enthusiasm for what you do, and truly caring about your players.

## Bernadette Locke-Mattox
HEAD WOMEN'S COACH,
AND FORMER PITINO ASSISTANT AT THE UNIVERSITY OF KENTUCKY

# STEP 7

## THRIVE ON PRESSURE

One second to play, your team is down by a single point, and you're at the free-throw line to shoot one and one. Twenty thousand fans are in the stands, the game is on national television, and all the eyes are on you. Make the first shot, and your team ties the game. Make them both, and your team wins. But miss the first shot and not only does your team lose the game, you are the goat.

This is the classic pressure situation, and every youngster who ever dribbled a ball in the backyard or on the playground has fantasized about being the player who toes that stripe on the foul line, the outcome of the game hanging in the balance.

I must have played out that scenario a thousand times when I was a kid. Everyone who ever played basketball did. And while very few of us ever actually get to that situation, for those few moments when we were kids we were brave and fearless, unafraid to accept the risk, willing to shoulder all the responsibility.

In those moments we stood toe to toe with failure, and we stared that demon down.

Why did we, as youngsters, constantly put ourselves into the most pressure-packed situations?

Why were we always putting pressure on ourselves on the free-throw line with one second to go? Or counting down the last five seconds as we launched a twenty-footer for the win? Or hitting a dramatic bottom-of-the-ninth home run that earned our team a victory?

Did we do these things because we all wanted to be the hero?

That's part of it. We all dream of being lifted onto the shoulders of our teammates and carried off the field of battle, surrounded by a mob of excited fans chanting our name. We all dream about getting the praise of our peers, the recognition that we have done something important, and we have done it well. We all want to feel important, have those moments we once only fantasized about actually come true.

But I don't believe that's the only reason why we placed ourselves in those situations. I believe there's a much deeper reason, one we probably didn't even understand at the time: We all wonder just how we *would* perform when the pressure is real rather than imagined.

Would we come through like we always do in our fantasies? Or would we get tagged with that most dreaded of all labels: a choker?

These are questions that are always with us, however subliminally.

How will I react when faced with a situation filled with pressure and uncertainty? Will I hold up my end? Will I perform admirably? Will I be a choker?

These are the questions we all want to be able to answer.

As a child, we envisioned performing in the adult world as some great new adventure. We weren't worried about pressure then; we only saw wondrous opportunities to prove ourselves. We closed our eyes and saw ourselves doing all kinds of amazing things.

But as you grow older and see your weaknesses, you start to lose confidence. You falsely assume that weakness in one area carries over to all aspects of yourself. The result is that you start to see pressurized situations become opportunities to fail, rather than opportunities to succeed. Worse, you compound the pressures in your life from work and home by piling responsibility on top of responsibility. Eventually, you start seeing this as one big mess, like a mountain you couldn't possibly climb, rather than a series of actions to be taken one step at a time.

That childlike wonder you once had is long gone.

You have begun to doubt yourself, and that doubt is one of the ingredients that leads to eventual failure. You have started to think of all the things you can t do, rather than all the things you can do. You now see pressure as some enormous obstacle, the boulder that you must somehow push up the hill, something that is going to crush not only your performance but also your spirit. All too often it becomes a self-fulfilling prophecy.

You need to rediscover your childlike wonder at being able to handle a pressure situation. You need to look at tomorrow with eager anticipation rather than fear. You need to once again feel that the world is full of possibilities—not that the world is oppressive and only going to strangle your dreams. But in order to do that, you must understand the difference between pressure and fear.

## STRESS VERSUS PRESSURE

My formula for handling pressure situations is simple: I consider pressure to be an ally and stress to be the enemy.

It's a philosophy I follow in both my personal life and my professional life as a basketball coach. Yes, pressure is always there in some form. It's in all of our lives, whether in the workplace or in our personal lives. It's a part of contemporary life, the product of our fast-paced jingle-jangle culture. To deny it is simply kidding ourselves. But we cannot allow it to control our performance in a negative way.

Most people will tell you that there's good pressure and there's bad pressure. I don't believe that. Pressure in and of itself is neutral. It's how you choose to view it that determines whether it's good or bad. If you use it to your advantage it's good pressure. Let it control you and it becomes bad pressure, or stress.

Just like with having a positive attitude, you have a choice every day in how you deal with pressure. You can either see it as something that's stimulating and exciting—something you can use as your ally—or you can worry about it and have it negatively affect your performance. It's up to you.

There are a lot of people who try to deny that pressure exists. Either that or they try to downplay it. Both strategies are losing ones.

You have to recognize it and prepare for it. It's like people who use vitamin C in an attempt to ward off colds as winter nears compared to the people who wait until they get the cold first before they start taking it. One group has prepared for the potential attack of a cold; one hasn't. It's the same thing with pressure. The more prepared you are the better you will handle it.

But pressure itself is not the enemy.

Stress is the enemy.

And stress appears when you're not prepared, not focused on your job. It shows up when you're cutting corners and looking for shortcuts.

Remember when you were in school and you had a big test that day, but you knew you didn't study enough? You knew you weren't prepared. That was stress, and you knew back then it was the enemy. Remember when you first had to speak in public, the dread you felt? That was stress, too, for you knew you had neither the skills nor the confidence to do it properly. You knew then that stress was the enemy.

Stress occurs when you are being asked to do something you're not sure you can do. From driving on icy roads, to having to do all your Christmas shopping in one day because you left it all to the last minute, to having to work all weekend to finish a work project, you feel stress because you know either that you're not fully prepared or that you've left yourself too little time to do things.

Stress also lessens your confidence. Because of this, you cannot possibly reach the proper level necessary to achieve success. When stress becomes a factor you make bad decisions. You don't perform well. You feel anxious. When stress comes into play you choke.

Again, let's use the example of being ill-prepared to take a big test. Because you know you're ill-prepared it's impossible to have confidence in your ability to do well on the test. Why should you have confidence? It goes back to what I said earlier in the book: You can't fool that person in the mirror. You know you're not prepared. You know you have no reason to feel confident. Enter stress.

When people are under stress you often see a shoddy performance from them. The stress gets in the way of being totally focused, to the point that they are simply not able to operate at optimum levels.

Stress also causes doubt. It makes you wonder whether you can get the job done. It makes you exaggerate the repercussions of a failure. It makes you think of failure instead of success. It makes you expect to fail.

If you watch and observe people in business you can often see who is under stress rather than pressure. It's the people who are irritable and short-tempered. The people who seem to view their work as some terrible burden, who move through the workplace joyless and obviously unhappy. The people who never seem to be having any fun. The people who seem to have *stress* all but stamped on their foreheads.

They are the people who drink too much. They bring their problems home with them. They have mood swings. They get easily frustrated. Eventually, their lifestyle itself becomes stressful, which only compounds the problem.

You know them. They're all around you every day.

These people often try to mask their stress by knocking their opposition. Their negative behavior forces them to try to denigrate their competition through negative statements and comments. Instead of promoting their own product, they attempt to show they're better than their competition by creating negative feelings about their competition. They're the ones who always are griping about other people in the office, as if by somehow denigrating others they cast themselves in a more favorable light.

This type of behavior is short lived, though, and without question it's counterproductive. People eventually see through this approach. They realize that if that salesperson's product is really strong there would be no reason to do anything other than compare it to the competition's.

Certainly you have to confront your competition, whether

it's a competitor, an opponent, or simply some obstacle you perceive to be in the way of reaching your goals. Not by denigrating that competition, but by trying to be better.

How do you do this?

By being truthful, and by creating a measuring stick that keeps you to a higher standard than your competitor. You're keeping the pressure on, but not letting the poison of stress pervade your attitude.

In recruiting, I try to avoid mentioning the other schools I'm competing against until the right time comes—when the recruit has narrowed his list down to a few schools. At that time I share information, but preface it by praising the opposition for being organized and efficient. Then I tell the recruit that it's now time to take a close look at each school's roster and see how he stacks up at his position. Which school offers him the best chance of getting his share of playing time? If one of our opponents has a lot of players at that position we point that out. We try to give the recruit information that will benefit our situation.

But we don't recruit by denigrating another school.

You can sense the negative coach—the one who's operating under negative stress—a mile away. There's not only a look of desperation about him, you can smell it in his presentation. He spends most of his time defending himself, while he knocks everyone else. This defense mechanism prevents him from making pressure an ally. Invariably, when he goes into a recruit's home for the final presentation, very often the defining moment that determines who gets the recruit and who does not, his stress will be showcased. That stress will almost always lead to failure.

And stress often occurs when you have not prepared properly.

The student who does not study and arrives for the exam

ill-prepared understands all too well that pressure is not his ally. The saleswoman who sneaks away in the afternoons to play golf knows the same thing. The person who is undisciplined and unstructured, with fuzzy goals and no plan of attack, certainly knows pressure is not a friend.

All of these people intuitively know—even if they can't articulate it—that any kind of pressure is going to knock their fragile world into a thousand tiny pieces. They know that any kind of pressure is instantly going to turn into stress.

Why?

Because they have not prepared themselves to handle it. So when any form of pressure arrives, it quickly causes doubt; that doubt lingers, and inevitably turns into stress. There's no escaping it.

But you also must keep things in perspective. Dealing with everyday problems is not like being in the military, which often deals with life-and-death situations; not like being a surgeon, who often has to perform with the highest stakes imaginable hanging in the balance. Instead, most of us are simply trying to be more successful in our lives.

You also must remember that stress is not just happening to you alone. You're not an island. Stress happens to all of us, for the simple reason that it's part of competition and part of being in the workplace. It's also often cyclical in nature, so that when it's happening to you, you can usually take some consolation in the fact that it will undoubtedly lessen, it's not always going to be so severe.

When stress does become a factor, though—when you're not motivated or excited about facing pressure—it's time to reevaluate the situation.

What's making you nervous and apprehensive? Why have doubt or negative beliefs entered your mind?

Certainly we all have periods of anxiety. We all have times

when the butterflies are in our stomachs. We wouldn't be human if we didn't. But doubt is something else again. Doubt is a crippler. Doubt is a negative. Doubt is one of the main paths on the highway to failure. You must do everything you can do to get doubt out of the equation.

Sure there are periods of uncertainty when you face a pressurized situation. But uncertainty doesn't have to translate into failure. All uncertainty means is you don't know what lies ahead.

The art of keeping things in perspective is a key element in battling stress.

Here are a few other habits to help you minimize stress in your life.

▶ Believe in your discipline. The more stressful the situation the more you must rely on the essential building blocks I've been talking about throughout this book.

▶ Don't confuse yesterday's pressure or tomorrow's pressure with today's pressure. Live for the moment you're facing. Take care of today, and tomorrow becomes easier to deal with. Don't waste precious energy worrying about what you have to do tomorrow. It's like the person who doesn't sleep well because he's worried about the future, and then he can't perform well today either because he's too tired. This is self-defeating.

It's human nature to initially panic when faced with a big project, for example. As the old adage says, "You look down all the road and all you see is more road." All this does is heighten stress.

Instead, break the project down into small, achievable

segments. It won't seem as overwhelming. It's the same principle as dealing with today's pressure instead of worrying
about tomorrow's. You want to be looking at small, achievable
goals that lead to larger goals, regardless of the task.

► Don't let people tell you what you can't do. Again,
we've talked about this before, but in stressful times
it's even more important. Only allow people to influence you when they can help you in a positive way.

► Spend more time doing and less time complaining.
Too often, people who feel stress start complaining
about how much pressure they're under. This is all
wasted energy, energy that could better be used for
something else.

► Stay positive under pressure.

I see Converse as a good example of how a company
should deal with stress. When I was a kid, every basketball
player wore Converse sneakers, usually their "Chuck Taylor"
model. All this, of course, was before anyone ever heard of
Nike, or Adidas, or Reebok, or any of the other companies
that now compete in the sneaker market. In the last five years
Converse has gone through troubled times because they
weren't doing the research and developing the product that
their competitors were. The people at Converse would leave
work each day wondering whether they could compete with
Nike, Reebok, or Adidas. No wonder. They realized they
hadn't kept up with the times. That they had changed management as frequently as one changes clothing. Their continu-
ity was not intact.

Sometimes change helps make pressure an ally, and
that's what's now happening at Converse. Their management

team is now intact and is probably stronger than ever. Their "back to tradition" shoe, bringing the leather Chuck Taylor model back into play, is certainly going to help their cause. Good pressure has now rejuvenated Converse. And the stress of being inferior is no longer lingering. Yes, they realize that at this point Nike is not in their immediate reach. But they see themselves as becoming more competitive in the marketplace, more successful.

Why?

Because instead of succumbing to stress, they applied pressure to their company; and that pressure is bringing out the best in everyone from research to sales.

## WHAT ARE YOUR PRESSURE POINTS?

There's no question that my Kentucky team faced an unbelievable amount of pressure last year. In the fall of 1995, we went into the season as everybody's number one, the consensus choice to win the national championship. There were even some basketball experts who said our second team was good enough to be ranked in the Top 10. Kentucky fans, desperate for their first NCAA championship since 1978, felt from day one that anything short of a national title would be a failure. "Win it all" was about the only thing my players, my coaches, and I heard as soon as we came back to school in September.

And this was all happening in Lexington, where the success of Kentucky basketball is supposed to be as certain as death and taxes.

The question for me as a coach was, How do we deal with this?

It would have been foolish for me to tell my players there was no pressure on them. Of course there was pressure on them. They knew that. They read the pre-season basketball magazines that virtually all had us picked number one in the country going into the season. They heard it from the other students. They heard it from everybody they talked to, an endless chorus.

So I decided before the season started to publicly embrace the pressure. I told my players that, yes, there was pressure on them and, yes, there was pressure on me. There was pressure on us because we represented the University of Kentucky. There was pressure on all of us because of all the lofty expectations. There was pressure on us that said that if we didn't win the national championship we were going to be asked to explain why we had failed.

Maybe more important, there was the pressure we had put on ourselves because we also knew we were the best team in the country, in terms of both talent and depth. We also felt we deserved victory because we all had worked so hard in preparing for the season.

But, as you know, there are two kinds of pressure: There's good pressure and there is bad pressure. Good pressure makes you better focused, more motivated. Bad pressure makes you feel anxious, afraid to fail.

I truly believe that we were able to win the national championship because we as a team came to understand the difference between good pressure and bad pressure. We were able to take the pressure we felt and make it work for us, by making us more focused, more committed to our goals. By realizing that when you're trying to be great, you need that great effort every day. It's that sense of discipline that prevents stress from making an appearance.

The first thing we did was create short-term goals for ourselves. We wanted to be the best half-court defensive team in the country. We wanted to lead the country in causing the most number of turnovers by our opposition. We wanted to be a great rebounding team.

Because it's very difficult to maintain excellence as an abstraction, we needed those specific short-term goals we could work on every day. Those short-term goals gave us something we could focus on daily as we continued to pursue our long-term goal of winning a national championship.

This was reinforced even more late in the season during our championship drive, when we knew we were getting closer and closer to our goal. We again talked about the pressure that was on us. Again, we did not pretend the pressure didn't exist, but talked about how we could make it work for us. Again, we embraced it and viewed it as a friend, not as some enemy.

We decided we'd treat every day as if it were our last game, all the while trying to be the best we could possibly be. We decided we would never take anything for granted, that we would try to live in the present tense and savor the great ride we were on. We decided every night out we would try to rise to an all-time level of performance, and that if we lost, it would be because the other team was better, not because we had let the pressure we were facing become stress and have it affect our performance.

The result?

This got everybody to respond, to understand his role. Most important, I believe it got everybody to realize what was at stake.

That's what good pressure is all about.

Pressure is a motivating force. It helps you run faster, jump higher, play better defense. It makes you focus in on your opponent and put out maximum effort. To execute at high efficiency.

We all have pressure points.

With my Kentucky team it was living up to other people's expectations. But they took that as a challenge, rather than shying away as if it were an impossibility. They saw what they had to do to control the pressure and did the necessary work.

So you must identify what the pressures in your life are and try to make those pressures work for you, rather than inhibit you.

Rather than perceiving responsibilities as pressure points, you need to take a cold hard look at what's actually causing the pressure. For instance, that report you have due Monday morning on the boss's desk isn't your pressure. Neither is the fact that you promised to take your kids away camping when you should be finishing up your report. These responsibilities are just part of life, so you can't blame your being overwhelmed or "my job's too hard," or "my kids don't understand that I can't do this."

What's really the pressure is time and how you handle it. Maybe you're going to need some help from your family and your friends to solve the problem. Maybe you're going to have to reassess the other things you are doing in your life.

Regardless, you need to see how you manage time as an area for improvement, not your work or your family. And then work on a solution from there. Learning how to manage pressure turns into simply becoming more organized and being able to prioritize your responsibilities.

Let's say, for example, you have so many things to do every day that you always feel harried, always feel rushed. The feeling that there's no time to enjoy anything because your plates are too full. This is a common complaint, something everyone feels at one time or another.

How do you cope with this? What do you do?

One remedy is to truly make sure you're organizing your time efficiently. Like I discussed earlier, write things down.

Prioritize them. What things definitely have to be done today, and what things can be put off?

Then do triage on the tasks you must get done today. Again, try to do the more unpleasant tasks early in the day, not only freeing up the rest of the day for more pleasant things, but also alleviating some of the pressure as soon in the day as possible.

Prioritizing also makes you focus more on what you have to do that day. That, in itself, invariably makes you better at performing those tasks. Knowing you are doing them better raises your self-confidence because there are few better feelings than coming through in a pressurized situation, whether you are at the free-throw line at a dramatic moment or simply operating the most efficiently you can during a demanding day.

This is the way you make pressure work for you and become your ally. This is when pressure makes what you do more fun. It makes all that pain of repetition and practice worth the price you've paid in sweat and toil and hard work.

Pressure becomes a negative only if you let it.

## WE MUST PREPARE FOR PRESSURE

The weekend golfer who goes out in the practice round and shoots an excellent score often starts to doubt whether he or she can do it again the next day when the real tournament starts.

Not Jack Nicklaus.

The great ones don't have those doubts, don't yield to the pressure.

Why?

I know what you're going to say. You're going to say Jack Nicklaus is a great golfer while the weekend golfer is not. Certainly that's true. But it's more than that.

The great ones also have prepared for pressure with countless hours of practice. When they were youngsters, alone in their backyards with just their dreams, they probably sank a thousand putts, envisioning themselves winning the Masters. Now, many years later, when faced with the real thing, they know they've prepared for the moment. They have paid their dues through their work ethic, the right technique, the countless repetitions, the perfect practice. They have worked hard for this day, this moment.

So now pressure becomes their caddy, the one that walks behind them, makes them focus more intently, understand the significance. And because they're risk takers, with a high sense of self-esteem, because they deserve victory, they are ready to take that next big step.

We often hear in sports that certain athletes are "pressure players," that they're tough in the clutch. Jerry West—the current general manager of the Los Angeles Lakers—was one of the greatest basketball players of all time and was known as "Mr. Clutch." He not only made the big shot throughout his career but wanted to take the big shot.

Why?

Not just because a great athlete like Jerry West wanted that moment to be his alone. It goes deeper than that. Above anything else, the great players feel their talents and the repetition of their practice enables them to succeed in that particular situation. They never look at missing that shot as being stressful. They understand that missing shots is all part of the game. However, because of their discipline and the self-confidence they've developed by all their perfect practice, they feel that percentage-wise they are going to hit more than they miss. That confidence is why they're willing to take that shot. They don't fear missing.

It all goes back to practice, to creating good pressure for yourself. Once you've done everything to prepare yourself, you eventually realize you're ready for that big moment, regardless of what it is.

You can believe that when Michael Jordan steps on a basketball court he not only feels he's the best player on that court but also expects his team to win. This isn't something that develops minutes before the game starts. This is a constant in every practice. Michael pushes all of his teammates, gets them to focus on the next opponent by practicing harder than anyone on the court. He is famous for it. He expects to be successful because he has paid the price to be successful. He deserves victory, and he knows it.

Those great athletes perform the task of winning each day by applying pressure to themselves to perform at the highest level possible. This daily ritual makes them what they are on game day. They have the talent. They've prepared for the moment. Now they live for the pressure.

That's what great entertainers do. They know that the performance is the reward for all the long hours of preparation. So they don't see being on stage as stress. And though it may be a certain form of pressure to be on stage performing for others, they, too, live for that pressure.

That's what you must do too.

You must have faith that your work ethic and your discipline have prepared you to be successful. You must understand that pressure only heightens your senses, provides the climate for you to perform better than you have in the past. Your preparation allows you to do this.

I always marvel at people who say, "We're not going to worry about what our opposition does. We're just going to execute and worry about what we do." I know that as a basketball coach I love to play any team whose coach has that philosophy, because we'll win 95 percent of the time.

Thorough preparation always gives you a big edge, regardless of the arena you're performing in. Knowing what your competition is thinking, or what they are about to do, is a tremendous advantage.

I've had teams where we've been slow afoot, small in stature, and yet we were able to rise to such a high level that we were called great defensively. Our edge was our preparation. During those times, we designed our game plan to force our opponents to take quick shots, which leads to poor percentage shots. We couldn't have done that without extensive and in-depth preparation.

It's all about preparing to face pressure.

By being unaware of your competition, you are simply inviting surprise and thus inviting stress. Preparation and research are two of the keys of staying away from stressful moments. Yes, you must be concerned with how you perform. But you better know what your opposition is doing, too.

Knowing these things is one more step in being prepared, and being prepared is one of the ways to combat stress. You're confident of your abilities. You're confident of your plan of attack. You're confident you can handle whatever is thrown in your path.

If you are not prepared—if you are seeing this pressure for the first time—you start to rely on guesswork, never a good situation to be in.

You are looking for a competitive edge, regardless of what you are doing. So it's really very simple: The better prepared you are for any situation, the more you believe you can succeed. The more you *will* succeed.

## APPLY THE PRESSURE TO YOURSELF

Look at any group of weekend golfers, regardless of their handicaps, and you will see a different intensity about them if they are playing for money. The amount is insignificant. Even if it's only a two-dollar Nassau, you will undoubtedly see much more focus than you would if there was no money involved.

Why?

The competition.

The competition tests your game. Having something at stake tests your game. And that pressure makes you grip the club a little differently every time you swing. It makes you focus. It makes you take nothing for granted. It makes you care.

So it's important that you don't fear pressure: You should embrace it. It brings out the best in all of us. You want it every day of your working life. You want to feel that each day you are under a microscope, that you are involved in something that's important.

When you're playing a game or competing head-to-head against a rival in business, the situation itself automatically pressures you to perform your best. When you're playing for a hard-driving coach or working for a tough boss, you will often be pressured to achieve at a high level. In fact, one of my maxims as a coach is "Apply the Pressure," because I strongly believe that you always get more out of people when you demand more.

But what do you do in situations where no one is expecting very much from you? Do you consider yourself lucky and coast, trusting that success will come to you in due course?

No, because that's not how success happens. Real greatness always occurs in response to intense pressure. Coasting and a belief in your inevitable good fortune bring mediocrity; hard work, constant striving, and fear of failure bring success.

Did you get that last one? You should fear failure: It's one of the secret ingredients of success. Ask just about any successful player, coach, or businessperson. If he or she is honest, that person will admit it: Fear of failure can be a master motivator, a big part of what drives him or her to succeed.

When the pressure is on, we're all at least a little afraid of failing. But don't be afraid of fear. Embrace it. Use it. Turn it to your advantage.

If nobody's demanding very much of you, follow my maxim: Apply the Pressure. But apply it to yourself. Learn how to do that, and you can succeed in almost any situation. Set higher standards for your own performance than anyone around you, and it won't matter whether you have a tough boss or an easy one. It won't matter whether the competition is pushing you hard, because you'll be competing with yourself.

By putting yourself into a competitive posture even when trying to achieve your very personal and individual goals, you can use pressure itself as a standard for how well you need to perform. If you just tell yourself, "I want to lose ten pounds," without psyching yourself up for that goal as if it were a contest, then it remains a fairly boring, uninspirational target. But if you turn up the pressure and tell yourself that losing the ten pounds is a critical step to your self-improvement and that you'd better do it or else, then you've jump-started your attitude and, probably, your results.

This self-directed pressure applies to all situations. If you find yourself facing pressure at work, at home, anywhere, you don't want to minimize it, you want to turn it up. This keeps you constantly excited and energetic and eager to succeed.

## Key Points for Step 7

Childlike wonder at accomplishment can charge you up for accomplishment. Rekindle the thrill of performing under the gun. You must recognize the difference between pressure and stress. Pressure makes you more focused and often is the environment for a great performance. Stress is the enemy. It robs you of your focus and inhibits your performance. Pressure is a negative only if you let it be.

△

Everyone has certain pressure points. The trick is to focus on yours and develop strategies to deal with them. You must prepare yourself for pressure. This takes a lot of the guesswork out of accomplishing your goals. The more you prepare the better qualified you are to handle pressurized situations. Pressure often brings out extraordinary results. If you learn how to embrace pressure and make it work for you, it can be a fertile climate in which accomplishment can grow.

△

When no one else is putting pressure on you, put it on yourself. Don't wait for pressure and the right circumstances to bring out the best in you. If nothing and no one are demanding a superior performance from you, demand it of yourself.

# APPLY THE PRESSURE
# IN EVERY PART OF
# YOUR LIFE

When I first met Coach Pitino I was going into my senior year at Providence College and he was coming off his job as an assistant with the Knicks.

I had been the leading scorer the previous year, so I guess you could say I was somewhat cocky. Truth is, I probably thought I was a better player than I really was, like a lot of players do. But from day one Coach preached to us how we all had to think team first, rather than think as a collection of individuals. He kept stressing how important the team concept was, and that individual awards are always secondary to what the team does.

We all had different personalities and came from different backgrounds. But he had a knack for dealing with you in a team context.

In the beginning we all thought he was crazy. I remember that Harold Starks—who was another player—and I would just look at each other.

But each week we started to see ourselves improve and then you start to believe. Eventually, you start to believe in yourself and then it becomes magic.

Another thing he did was put everything on the line when we were on the court. We had state-of-the-art drills, the best conditioning, the most effective fundamental drills. But what both impressed and inspired me the most was that, yes, he was gung-ho about his players on the court, but he was equally gung-ho about us off the court. He wanted the same goals and fundamentals for us as young men.

That was the first time I had ever seen that. Most coaches wanted you to work hard on the court and win as many games as possible. Coach Pitino wanted to also see us break out of the eggshell and mature as young men.

He taught us to have respect for everyone. For teammates, media, parents, opponents, the priests on campus. Everyone. He also taught us that you get out of life what you put into it. You must put in 110 percent every day. You have to be consistent in your work ethic, and that you work as hard the last minute as you did the first.

These are lessons I try to practice every day of my life. I am currently in the process of starting my own business, and I hear his voice in my head virtually every day. About having a work ethic. About trying to be the best you can possibly be. About getting up early and staying late. All the fundamental things that I took from him and incorporated into my life. I take all the team goals he always talked about and apply them to my business.

He also told me when I was a senior that even though I was good enough to play professionally in Europe, I was not good enough to ever play in the NBA, so that I should pour my energies into a business career and get started on it right away. Then he helped me get a job with Coca-Cola.

I look at Coach Pitino as a superhero. I have the utmost respect for him. He's a person I like to be around, a person I admire and want to be like. He changed my life, and even now it's like he's still coaching me, even though it's a decade later.

## Donnie Brown
PRESIDENT OF NATIVE AMERICAN BEVERAGES
AND FORMER PITINO PLAYER

# STEP 8

# BE FEROCIOUSLY PERSISTENT

A man is a hero, not because he is braver than anyone else, but because he is brave for ten minutes longer.

—Ralph Waldo Emerson

On the road to deserving victory, we have learned that we have to develop strong self-esteem, maintain a positive attitude, and set demanding goals for ourselves. We have learned that we must acquire good habits and skills and learn from people who are older and wiser than we are. We have learned that we must be able to make pressure work for us, without allowing stress to cripple our efforts.

Now comes the hard part.

The part that determines who is actually going to stick to his or her organized plan of attack, and who is going to fall by the wayside.

What's the key?

Persistence.

Sheer persistence.

There's no real mystery to it. No secret blueprint. Nothing that's all that complicated. Simply the awareness that after you establish the work ethic, and after you've started to master the techniques, the real struggle is just beginning.

It's persistence that makes you great. It's persistence that allows you to reach your dreams. It's persistence that enables you to perform at your fullest potential.

There might be no better example of persistence than Thomas Edison. A prolific inventor, Edison received 1,033 patents, including ones for the phonograph, microphone, and the incandescent electric lamp. He certainly had more than his share of great victories along the way.

But think of how many failures Edison had, too. Literally thousands. To his great credit, though, Edison didn't see them as such. When reminded that he had failed something like 25,000 times while experimenting with the storage battery, Edison supposedly responded by saying, "No, I didn't fail. I discovered 24,999 ways that the storage battery does not work."

What a marvelous outlook.

An outlook we all can learn something from.

The thing to remember is that anybody can be great and perform to the hilt for a day, a week, even a month. We know people in all walks of life who get on a great roll, ride the adrenaline high, and wonderful things begin to happen left and right. Then, all too often, they begin to feel content. They've made a change, right? They've become more successful, right? So why not relax and enjoy it, bask for a moment in the newfound success?

We see the pattern all the time. It's the person who goes on an exercise program, does it for six months, begins to both look and feel better, and then feels satisfied. Now that "I've made some progress," he or she says, "I don't have to work as hard."

But the people who will ultimately pull ahead and wind up on top are the ones who make personal excellence a lifelong commitment. These are the people who go after it day after day. They keep raising the bar, becoming neither discouraged by pitfalls nor complacent by success. They understand that the pursuit of excellence is a marathon, not a sprint. It's a journey, not some little day trip. It's a lifetime quest, not some fashionable trend to be tried for a few months only to be discarded when the next fad comes along. They understand that the quest to be the very best they can—to reach the fullest extent of their mental, physical, and psychological potential—has no time limit on it.

The dictionary says *persistence* is "refusing to give up, or let go. Persevering obstinately. Continuing despite opposition." In sports parlance, persistence means hanging in the game, not tossing in the towel, refusing to quit. In life, it's the same thing.

One thing I've noticed in all my years of coaching is that the most successful athletes, the most successful people in all walks of life, in fact, have one thing in common—they persist. They refuse to let anyone tell them their dreams can't come true. They never waver in their belief in themselves. They refuse to be denied.

They also realize success is not going to happen overnight.

I have a young man from Canada on my team now named Jamaal Magliore. Although he's a freshman he is already starting for us—unusual for the Kentucky team—and is one day going to be an outstanding player. But in one of the games this past December he didn't play particularly well and failed to score. The next day in practice I could tell he was a little down.

"I don't understand this," he said. "I should be doing better."

"Jamaal," I said, in front of the team. "I don't understand what I did for fifteen years, back when I was a young coach. All those summers when I traveled around to all those basketball camps giving lectures. All those times when I was an assistant at Syracuse and I would drive all day to some place like Cape May, New Jersey, see a kid play, then drive back all night. Or all those times when I was at Boston University driving a Renault Le Car on recruiting trips, all the while wondering whether the car was going to hold up during the recruiting season or fall apart by the side of the road and leave me stranded.

"I don't know why I did all that. I just should have become the coach of the Knicks when I was twenty-two and the coach at Kentucky when I was twenty-four. I should have just told people that I didn't want to do all those things I did for fifteen years. I don't know why I paid all those dues."

By this time I could see Jamaal was a little confused, not quite sure where I was going with this.

"Look at you, Jamaal. You're a freshman. Last year you played in a league where there was very little competition, and you've always played basketball about four months a year and took the other eight months off. But now that you're at a level where everyone works ferociously on their game twelve months a year, you're not having success, and you can't understand it."

The point—which Jamaal eventually came to understand—is that he hasn't come anywhere near to paying his dues yet; and until he does that, how can he expect to be successful every night?

He hasn't learned yet that it's all about persistence, that until you prove that you can stick it out over time you really haven't proved anything. He hasn't yet learned that simply because he's now worked harder for the past four months than he's ever worked in his life, he still doesn't deserve victory. He's on his way, certainly. He's on the right path. But he's nowhere near there yet.

For he hasn't proved he's got persistence.

The persistent person raises the bar to seemingly unreachable heights, then establishes the methods necessary to reach those heights. The persistent person purposely sets tough goals because he or she understands that making it only part way is ultimately empty and unsatisfactory. The persistent person knows that letting up will only get him or her back to the starting point.

We constantly see examples of outwardly motivated people falling off just when they need to keep getting better.

We all know talented people who never seem to reach their potential because they don't keep at what they're trying to accomplish: the good students who see their grades slide for no apparent reason, the salesman who has a great two weeks but fades off the second half, the athlete who reaches a plateau, the gifted person in the workplace who never seems to reach her potential. These people have great early success, then seem to fade into oblivion.

Those who lack persistence start out with the best intentions, but they eventually drift. Or else they move from one new thing to the other, hoping that something will hold their interest. They lose their focus and let their short-term goals slide. Inevitably, the possibility of achieving their dreams becomes unlikely.

This trait is quite characteristic, for example, of people who are constantly changing careers. They invariably start out with good intentions, become enthusiastic about their new job and feed off this momentum for a while to perform well. But when this newness wears off and they realize they aren't incredibly committed to sticking with that job in the long term, their success begins to wane and they start to fail.

Why?

Because they are not persistent.

They get sidetracked, or they get distracted. They might have everything else going for them. A strong work ethic, the right methods, all the best intentions. But they don't have persistence. And that lack of persistence is what ultimately prevents them from reaching their dreams.

We all know talented people who seem reluctant to take the extra step that can make them great at what they do. They may be very good at what they do; they may even love what they do. Yet they are unwilling to take it to that next level. Like the student who is content to make the honor roll, instead of putting in that added effort that might result in high honors. Like the salesman who reaches his quota then starts to relax. Like the employee who does everything that's asked of her, yet everyone knows that she could do more if she only pushed herself a little harder. These people find their comfort zone and are content to remain there.

Take the case of Delray Brooks, for instance.

Delray is one of my assistant coaches at Kentucky, someone who played for me at Providence College and who is going to make a fine head coach some day. Right now he is someone who will do everything I ask him to do, and he will do it with dedication, competence, and commitment. If I tell him to make fifteen phone calls he will make all fifteen, no matter how late he has to stay at work to do so. But he won't make the sixteenth. He won't make that extra step, and that's what I'm now trying to get him to do. To take what I tell him and move on from there with his own ideas and his own creativity. To be willing to take that next step, rather than merely be content doing what's expected of you.

And he's now taking that extra step, forming his own identity. He's traveled the road from ex-player to assistant coach to future head coach. We were about to lose Ron Mercer, a prized recruit, to Tennessee. Ron had heard all the recruiting pitches about as much as one could tolerate. Delray convinced me to hammer at it one more time. So I did, going to Oak Hill Academy in the foothills of Virginia, where I went to the blackboard in a classroom and pointed out in minute detail why the University of Kentucky was best suited for his future. Ron signed with us shortly after. Delray's insistence that we go after it one more time was the turning point to our attracting the top high school player in the country.

That's the kind of persistence you should be looking for: the kind that takes you above and beyond. The kind that's going to let nothing stand in the way of your success.

It was during the NCAA tournament in 1987, and my Providence team was playing Austin Peay. In retrospect, that might have been the game that changed the direction of my career. If we didn't win that game we didn't go to the Final Four. If we didn't go to the Final Four, I wouldn't become the Coach of the Year, probably wouldn't become the coach of the New York Knicks that summer.

On that afternoon in Birmingham, Alabama, we were down ten points with just five minutes to play, staring at a loss that would have ended our season. And as the team gathered around me in a time-out, tired, the panic becoming visible in their eyes, I knew I needed something special to spur them on.

So I started talking calmly, in a low voice.

"We probably are going to have to congratulate Austin Peay so you better start getting ready for it. They have outplayed you all afternoon. They have beaten your press. They have shut down your offense. They have been in control the entire game. They have been the better team.

"Some days it just doesn't happen," I continued, beginning to raise my voice. "Some days you try as hard as you can try, and you do everything right, but it's just not to be. It looks like this is one of those days. But there's one more thing you can do. Just one."

By this time I was screaming.

"For the next five minutes we can rip our hearts out and throw them on the floor. Just throw them on the floor and see what happens."

What happened?

We did rip our hearts out.

We made a miracle comeback and kept the season alive.

## GET THE PHD ATTITUDE

When I was helping Jamal Mashburn, one of my top players, find someone to manage his money a couple of years back, I was looking for someone who was conservative, who had a lot of experience, and who had withstood tough times. My research took me to a man named Mario Gabelli, who handles millions of dollars in corporate investments and university endowments.

Mario gave me a tour of his company in Rye, New York; he must have had between seventy-five and one hundred employees in the back room all handling various accounts. I asked him what he looked for in hiring people, how he created his employee base. Was it a Wharton diploma? Harvard Business School? What was it?

"I hire PHDs," he said.

"I don't understand," I said. "I would think in your business you would hire people with expertise in managing money, not Ph.D.s."

"Not in an academic sense," he said. "I'm looking for poor, hungry, and driven people."

I've never forgotten Mario's phrase, and now I, too, look for people who are poor, hungry, and driven.

Now I'm not talking about people being poor economically. I'm talking about being poor in terms of knowledge, about people who are constantly searching to learn more, to find more wisdom. And hungry people in this context refers to those with a tremendous desire to succeed, people who won't ever be satisfied with an ordinary level of accomplishment. And driven people are the ones who set ambitious goals and then pursue them with real ferocity.

For instance, there's no question that professional athletes in the last year of their contracts tend to be more driven and often have the best year of their whole contract. Why? Because they know that last season is the key to their next job, and they have more of a desire to do well.

But why do so many people have to be in the last year of their contract to put out the kind of great effort that leads to a great performance?

I've also seen what I call the New Year's Resolution syndrome. You know that one; it shows up in the person who says in the middle of November that come New Year's he is going on a diet to lose twenty pounds. He announces it to everyone: "After New Year's I'm going on a strict diet." Then he eats another cheeseburger and more fries because it's not New Year's yet.

The only problem is that between the middle of November and New Year's he gains ten more pounds.

What you have to do is make your New Year's resolutions 365 days of the year. The same resolve. The same determination. The same commitment. And do it on a daily basis. That's what persistent people do: They make every day a day for fulfilling their New Year's resolutions.

It shouldn't take being in the last year of your contract or a New Year's resolution to motivate you to be driven to succeed. All year round, the PHD attitude is a common denominator among almost all successful people, regardless of their occupation. These are the people who jump out of bed in the morning ready to accomplish more at work than they ever have before. They seem to have almost superhuman energy. They seem to have a boundless supply of curiosity, optimism, and drive. To all appearances, they could accomplish just about anything they set their minds to.

One foolproof indicator of people with a PHD attitude is great concentration. These highly motivated people are almost always deeply absorbed in what they're doing. I rarely look at the clock when I'm coaching, so engrossed am I in what I'm watching and teaching and learning about my team. I don't want the time to move by quickly. There's always too much to be done and too little time to do it in.

That's the attitude you must adopt every day of your working life. Poor, hungry, and driven. That's the message you have to be sending out to both your employer and your co-workers, this sense that nothing is going to get in the way of your success.

## "THE HARDER YOU WORK, THE TOUGHER IT IS TO SURRENDER"

Vince Lombardi said that in his heyday with the Green Bay Packers in the 1960s, and it's as true as ever.

Truly persistent people never give in to mental or physical fatigue.

Truly persistent people don't give in, period.

They understand their journey will not be made of shortcuts and easy targets. They always are striving to be the best they can be. Persistent people treat each day as a competitive game: prepared to win, with a never-give-up attitude.

They condition themselves to win.

They have that old-fashioned work ethic, and that's become their norm. They expect to work hard. They expect to put in the effort. And they expect to succeed. They don't go to bed at night worrying about failing. They go to bed at night thinking about getting up the next day and having another chance to succeed.

They go into a big exam knowing they're going to do well, because they're overprepared. They didn't cram at the last minute, so they don't arrive at the test anxious and full of doubt. They did everything they were supposed to do, and more. They know they're ready.

They're the ones who are supposed to run two miles, but do three instead. They're supposed to make ten calls a day; they make twelve. They're always going beyond what's expected of them, because they have conditioned themselves to. It's become part of who they are. They are not going to get distracted. They are not going to get sidetracked. They are not going to lose sight of their goals and let them slide.

Why?

That's simple.

Because they have worked too hard to get to where they are to stop now. They're not about to surrender. They're the people who lose a game only because time runs out on them, not because they doubt their plan or give less than their best effort. They're the people who get overlooked for the promotion, but come back the next day as committed and focused as ever, knowing that there's always going to be a tomorrow, and they are going to be ready for it.

They also understand that the more they run the race course the harder it is to quit the race. They've put so much effort into it. They know they can do it. They've been there before, so they know the distance, know the terrain. There is no way they are going to quit, because they know they can finish the race.

That's why our Kentucky team can handle it when we don't win, while other teams often get discouraged. If we lose a game, we still know that we put in the hours, the energy, the effort. We still know that we did everything we were capable of to prepare for that game. Sure, we're disappointed that on that particular night our opponent simply played better. But we know that we deserved to win, and we're eagerly awaiting the next time.

It's the people who know they don't deserve it who will surrender. The people who never have run the race before. The ones who have not conditioned themselves. These are the ones who won't stay the course.

To achieve peak condition, virtually all the great over-achievers I have known compete against themselves. They know competition is good, because it makes them perform better. So the best way of making sure that they're working their hardest is to play a game against themselves. Create their own Olympics, if you will.

How do you do this?

By setting up goals for yourself every day. Goals that you can reach and goals that tax you. Goals that you can strive for every day. Because that's what you're looking for: daily successes. A succession of daily successes that you can shoot for and measure up how well you did. Afterward—whether you've been to a job, a practice, or a treadmill—you must rate the game you just played.

How did you perform?

Was it pleasing? If so, why?

What was difficult? Why?

By rating your performance you instantly can see not

only what you have to do better but the pitfalls that wait for you along the way. This is your personal scorecard, your way of telling yourself whether you won or lost that day. And if you lost? If you are truly persistent, it only gives you more resolve not to lose tomorrow.

## BE FLEXIBLE

As tough as this sounds, our knowledge is becoming obsolete every day.

Do we need any better example than the proliferation of computers in the past decade? Now, if we're not computer literate, we're not only considered behind the times but will not even be ready to perform in the years ahead. Technology is just one of the things that is dramatically changing our work and our lives, and if we don't adjust we will quickly be left behind.

That was certainly true for me in the fall of 1986 when the three-point shot came into college basketball. All of us coaches knew it was destined to significantly alter the college game, but none of us really knew what radical impact it would have.

I was in my second year of coaching at Providence College then, and I remember writing on the blackboard before our exhibition game with the Russian National Team that in order to achieve what we wanted for that season, I felt we were going to have to lead the country in three-point shot attempts. Before that first game, I said we must attempt fifteen three-point shots per game, thinking not only that that was more than enough but that people would deem us revolutionary for launching them with such frequency.

By half-time, the Russians had put up twenty-one three-point attempts, while we had taken fifteen. All of a sudden, I realized my initial number was too small, that we needed to take more. We then pushed the number up to twenty-five a game, hoping to make at least eight.

As the season progressed I began to realize that many of the coaches we were competing against were not prepared to make that change. Certain people had developed old habits years back, and they were not ready to adopt this new philosophy into their strategy. They considered it too risky, low percentage, not worth the gamble. They preferred to stick with what they knew, what was comfortable for them. That's human nature. Given a choice, we'd all like to remain in our comfort zone as much as possible.

But it was obvious that this attitude was working to their detriment.

This can be true in the office as well.

You see it in certain people who always want other people to use the computer, to tackle the new technology. Why? Because new technology can be overwhelming, confusing, and frightening. However, by not learning the new tools that would help them to perform better at work, these people remain stagnant, refusing to adapt; and all because of the habits they've created in their lives that they are unwilling to break.

What eventually happened in college basketball was that the three-point shot came to be embraced by every coach, for the simple reason that coaches began looking at the numbers and reevaluating. What they eventually realized is that shooting 33 percent from the three-point line is just as productive as shooting 50 percent from the two-point line. Suddenly, three-point shots were flying all over the place, and college basketball was changed forever.

The same thing will happen with the technophobes in business: They too will realize they'll lose revenues and eventually their jobs if they hold out on learning new skills too late.

You must always readjust.

Readjust and develop a philosophy that allows you to stay ahead. Because if you're not staying ahead you're falling behind.

This is not always easy, for as the adage goes: "Old habits die hard."

We all know people so set in their ways it's as if they were cast in concrete. We also know people who seem to change their habits as frequently as they change their clothes.

Both extremes are dangerous; you have to moderate the methods that have worked well in the past with the ability to be flexible and responsible.

You, of course, need consistent good habits that you can repeat over time—your foundation of productive behavior.

But let's face it, repetition can lead to boredom. Human beings are not machines. We break down when we're over-taxed. We grow tired of the same things over and over, whether it's eating the same food, exercising on the same machine, or running over the same course every day.

No matter how excited you are when you begin a new challenge, boredom can eventually begin to undermine persistence. When boredom threatens your desire to keep working on something, you have to start looking for new ways to stimulate your mind, to make sure what you're doing is fun and interesting again. You must always keep searching for better ways to accomplish your goals, while at the same time taking care not to lose sight of the repetition necessary to take your performance to the highest level possible.

In your daily routine, in your quest for developing good, sound habits that can lift your performance, several factors should be considered:

> ▶ Old devices and methods must be thoroughly researched to make sure they're the most efficient way to make your day the most productive it can be.

▶ You must readjust when necessary, to keep your mind stimulated.

▶ You can't stay put and let your feet settle in concrete. You must keep cultivating new methods and new ways.

Being creative about solutions to problems gives you additional motivation to bring to what you do every day. Flexibility/adaptability is a habit that can be cultivated and can be critical to maintaining the enthusiasm you need for persistence. You have to look at each day as a new opportunity to change one thing about your life. This will keep time flying by, rather than just wanting the rest of the week to be over.

Unmotivated people generally see a huge division between their work and their play, their vocation and their avocation. Self-motivated people see little difference. They love what they do. They can't wait to get to work in the morning. They can't wait to get started. They are the ones who believe that there aren't enough hours in the day to accomplish the goals they're trying to reach.

## ELIMINATE *QUIT* FROM YOUR VOCABULARY

I liked going to the University of Massachusetts, but it wasn't easy for me. After my freshman year I was cocky and had a certain New York attitude. I was convinced that I was going to start on the varsity as a sophomore; but when practice began, I was playing behind two veteran guards, Mike Pagliara and John Betancourt, and I thought I was better than they were.

My first instinct was to quit, to transfer, but Ray Wilson, one of the assistant coaches, to whom I was close, talked me out of it. One day in practice I got into a fight with Pagliara, who broke his finger. "Now I'll start," I thought.

The next day I'm playing behind Betancourt, and eventually we get into a fight as well and wrestle to the ground. Betancourt now is hurt, too. "Now I'll definitely start," I tell myself. Jack Leaman, the head coach who was a disciplinarian from the old school, suspended me instead. I was devastated and wanted to transfer, but Wilson again talked me out of it. "You can't run away if you're a man," he told me. "It's time to grow up. To learn how to sacrifice yourself."

When I came back to the team the next year I was the thirteenth man, a pariah. The others on the team would run together; Leaman told me to run alone. Others would make mistakes and be ignored; I would make mistakes and be singled out. There wasn't a practice that went by when I didn't want to tell Leaman what he could do with his basketball team. But every day I vowed to stick it out, knowing that it had become a battle of wills. Four days before the first game I broke into the starting lineup. I felt as if I had survived boot camp. Then in the locker room, minutes before the first game, Leaman announced the starting lineup and I wasn't in it. I was crushed. I felt tears coming into my eyes. Would this never end? Hadn't I already proven myself? What more did I have to do?

Thirty seconds after the game started Leaman motioned for me to go into the game.

"It's over, Rick," Ray Wilson whispered as I walked by.

I didn't understand it at the time, but Jack Leaman made a man out of me. He shaped my life. And it's a lesson I've used often in my own coaching: taking on a player's individual will, his selfishness, and then molding him into someone who will be able to sacrifice himself for the good of the team.

But I almost quit, and I often wonder what would have happened if I did. Odds are it wouldn't have been good.

A lot of young coaches now try to model their systems on what we do at Kentucky: the same presses and the same offensive philosophies. But invariably they will say to me, "We do everything you do, with one exception. We can't get our players to work the way yours do. How do you get your players to work so hard?"

To us, working hard is the norm. That's the constant, the one thing we expect every day. I would be shocked if one of my teams didn't play hard.

And on those rare days when they don't, I ask myself why. Are we fatigued? Are we embracing success, which is a sure blueprint for eventual failure? Are we coming off a big game or is our next game too far away? Are we down on ourselves?

At such times I will take my team off the court, because my first rule is that when we step between the lines we have to deserve victory. Between those lines we must realize that the team is bigger than any individual, that it doesn't matter who gets the credit, that the only thing that matters is winning. Above all, we must give it everything we've got. We simply do not allow a subpar effort. Going only partway is tantamount to quitting, and we cannot quit.

A year ago, my son Michael, who had just graduated from high school, had to choose between two summer jobs. He could work either at my basketball camp or at one of the horse farms in the Lexington, Kentucky, area. It was his choice. He chose the horse farm, because he was tired of working my camps, and he thought he could make more money at the horse farm. But after only a few days he realized he hated it. Farm work is hard, and he was spending most of his time walking horses on a treadmill and shoveling manure. One day a couple of weeks into the summer he came to me and said he'd made a mistake and would rather work at my basketball camp.

I understood, but I told him that he'd made a commitment and now he was going to have to follow through with it, no matter how unpleasant. Quitting was not an option.

Sometimes, of course, we fail to accomplish our goals. But we have to remember that failure is a part of life and failure is only fertilizer for future success. I've often heard people say that failure teaches us nothing. I don't believe it. There are so many lessons we can learn from failure. Most of all, we learn what not to do. It's like the child who touches the hot stove, and then keeps doing it. The first time is part of the learning process. The second time it's stupid.

The only time failure is truly bad is if you use it as an excuse to quit.

Let's say, for instance, that you're up for a promotion that you've worked very hard for. And you don't get it. Now there are two basic ways to deal with that: You can let that disappointment eat away at you, spending a lot of time wondering why the other person was promoted over you and essentially take yourself out of the running for any other promotions right then and there. Or you can put your energy into preparing yourself for the next time around. You will soon realize that wasting time and energy focusing on that disappointment will cancel out all the other work you've done to get this far, and you might as well have quit.

The other potentially dangerous thing about failure is it can be distracting. So if you only focus on the fact that you failed and don't examine the reasons why you failed, it's likely that you'll fail again.

This is not to say there aren't pitfalls along the way. I've certainly seen people lose persistence because of failures both real and imagined—from being bested by their competition to the lack of instant gratification following a burst of hard work. But those who are persistent for that ten minutes longer will be the only ones around long enough to realize their dreams.

So how do you keep persisting when you face setbacks along the way?

Persistence is a direct result of the organizational chart you set up for yourself. I've never known a successful person who isn't organized. Being organized makes you stick to your plan of attack and acts as the lighthouse when you're navigating through stormy waters. By now, your attitude, your habits, and your work ethic are second nature, and you can now see why organizing your life around these ten steps is so critical. These ingrained patterns of behavior are allowing you to keep going, even as you want to quit. They enable you to seek out challenges rather than be afraid of them.

In my profession few things are more important than recruiting. If I'm going to be successful at the highest level, I have to have great players to work with. It's that way with all coaches. Recruiting is the lifeblood of our success, and every coach wants the kind of player that can take his or her team to the next level.

Recruiting is also tough, tiring, expensive, thrilling, and deflating. It can make you very high or very low. And I love it. Meeting the young men; getting to known them, their families, and their coaches; watching them play; trying to sell myself and the University of Kentucky; going head-to-head against other great coaches and schools. It's all the essence of competition, a part of the job I relish.

But it also takes great persistence. For in recruiting there are a lot more failures than successes. That's a fact, cold and hard. More times than not, the player you're after, the one you've been wooing for two or three years, chooses another school. That's just the way the job is. It's disappointing and difficult to accept sometimes when you lose a recruit you've worked so hard on, but you have to put it behind you and move on to the next player you're recruiting.

It's the same in the business world. Ask any salesperson.

No matter how successful he or she is, a salesperson will tell you that the failures far outnumber the successes. That's the way it is.

So why are such salespeople successful?

Simple.

They persist. They keep working at it. They refuse to quit. They know there are going to be failures, but they also know failures only make them tougher, more resilient. They know that failures are little more than potholes along the journey, something to ride over quickly, avoid the next time, and then keep going on their way.

## Key Points for Step 8

Anyone can be great and perform to the hilt for a day, a week, or a month. But if you want to be successful over the long haul you must be willing to stay the course.

△

PHDs will come out on top. Poor, Hungry, Drivens, that is.

△

Paying the price of hard work makes you less willing to surrender.

△

Don't get discouraged by stumbling blocks along the way. You must be flexible enough to readjust and move on, without getting sidetracked.

△

You must eliminate the word *quit* from your vocabulary. This is the essence of persistence. People who won't quit, don't.

# NEVER DOUBT THAT
# YOU CAN DO THE JOB

I remember Coach Pitino's first year at Kentucky when Kansas beat us by fifty-five points.

Despite being badly outplayed, we were within about six points with about three minutes to go in the first half. Then we just fell apart and were down something like twenty-five at the half. Coach really got on us about taking bad shots and not getting back on defense. After the game he really challenged us, telling us we played like a bunch of wimps. He was really hot.

But the next day he came out, talked to us for a while about the Kansas game, and then moved on. He treated it like it was just another game. He doesn't dwell on yesterday's loss. Instead, he's always looking forward to the next day, the next game. That's his NBA mentality. He takes a loss badly—for about thirty minutes. Then he's on to preparing for the next opponent.

I always felt he was a much better coach after we lost, or even after we won but had played poorly. The reason is because it gave him a better opportunity to motivate. A team that's winning big, really playing well is sometimes more difficult to motivate. That's because it's hard to get the players' attention. Coach is a great motivator when you're winning, but he's even better after a loss.

One thing I always loved about him is that he never holds grudges. He doesn't have a doghouse. He'll get on you hard, but once he gets his point across he moves on. Some coaches keep players in a doghouse for an entire season. You can't be successful that way. Coach Pitino understands that's what being a successful motivator is all about. Preach your message, teach, but don't dwell on the negative. Always accent the positive.

He knew that I was the type of person you have to stay on top of 85 percent of the time, because if I thought I was going good I would have a tendency to get lax.

He never told me how good I was. He never told me I played well when I had a good game. And that kept me always striving for excellence. The only thing he used to tell me is that with the ability I had there shouldn't be another point guard who could outplay me.

Coach is a very smart man who can read people very quickly. In my case, I was always a cocky player. I never doubted I could do the job. So the way Coach kept me in line—kept me from getting too full of myself—was by never telling me how good I was. He always stayed on me, but in a positive way. That kept me at a level key.

He also knew I was stronger mentally and emotionally than most of the guys on the team. Because of that, I was the one who got fussed at the most. It all goes back to his ability to read and understand the makeup of each player.

The first year he was the coach at Kentucky—a year in which we were supposed to be awful, but ended up .500—Coach knew that I was the only person on the team who could play effective man-to-man defense. Yet when things would break down defensively, when somebody else got beat, he jumped on me. He would make an example out of me, because he knew that some of the other guys couldn't take it, but that I could.

The primary thing I learned from Coach Pitino, though, was that you have to use every day of your life to be the best you can possibly be, no matter what you are doing. And that's 100 percent of the time. Not 80 percent. Not 90 percent. But always 100 percent. Never leave any room for error.

**Sean Woods**
FORMER UNIVERSITY OF KENTUCKY PLAYER,
NOW A SALES REPRESENTATIVE
FOR A LEXINGTON TELEVISION STATION

# STEP 9

## LEARN FROM ADVERSITY

As long as we maintain the right attitude and a certain amount of flexibility, we will be able to persist through the ups and downs we face in our day-to-day lives. If we're tough and driven and work harder than we ever have before, we'll keep that "damn the torpedoes" approach and focus on what we need to do, not what's getting in our way.

All of us ought to be able to brace ourselves for the predictable challenges and setbacks that crop up every day. I know, for instance, that while we can persuade great freshmen to come to Kentucky, we won't be able to get *all* of the best high school basketball recruits in the country to come to our school. I also know that we won't win every single game of the season. And you know that you can't win every single account you pitch to potential clients or always be the only one with a great idea or never be caught off guard by a competitor.

In other words, we can expect that life won't be perfect, and if we know this, we'll be able to avoid that impulse to quit.

But even if you are strong enough to persist through the obstacle course of life and work, sometimes you will encounter an adverse event that will completely knock you on your back. This may be an event out of your control that affects your life or health so profoundly that it may seem like the end of your dreams. Or it might be a complete and utter failure that devastates you, makes you question every single thing you have worked so hard to accomplish. Whether it's a financial loss, the loss of respect of your peers or loved ones, or some other traumatic event in your life, these major setbacks leave you doubting yourself and wondering if things can ever change for the better again.

Adversity happens to all of us, and it happens all the time. Some form of major adversity is either going to be there or else it's going to be lying in wait just around the corner. It's as much a part of life as the food we eat and the air we breathe. To ignore it is to succumb to the ultimate self-delusion.

But you must recognize that history is full of examples of men and women who achieved greatness despite facing situations so dire and hurdles so steep that so easily could have crushed their spirit and left them lying in the dust. Moses was a stutterer, yet he was called on to be the voice of God. Abraham Lincoln overcame a difficult childhood, depression, the death of two sons, and constant ridicule during the Civil War to become arguably our greatest president ever. Helen Keller made an impact on the world despite being deaf, dumb, and blind from an early age. Franklin Roosevelt had polio. So did Wilma Rudolph. Rocky Blier had a solid professional football career despite being wounded in Vietnam. Bill Clinton became the president of the United States, even though he once lost the governorship of Arkansas and thought his political career might be over forever.

There are endless examples, but you get the point.

These are people who not only looked adversity in the face but learned valuable lessons about overcoming the circumstances and were able to move ahead.

How did they do it? Through sheer will, hard work, an unwavering belief in themselves, and maybe most important of all, strength of character. Nothing more No magic potions. No miracles. No bolts of lightning that came down from the heavens and changed their lives.

These people simply told themselves that they couldn't say no.

Most of us, of course, will never achieve what Lincoln or Roosevelt achieved. Their legacy is tied up in the times in which they lived, the special circumstances that shaped them and led them on the path of public service. We are never going to be the president during a war. We won't be asked to hold a nation together during the most trying of times.

Yet that doesn't mean you can't greatly benefit from studying people who have displayed great character. It doesn't mean you can't try to learn how they developed the seeds of great character. It doesn't mean you can't take some of the same traits that made these people great and use those traits in your own life. And it certainly doesn't preclude us from trying to emulate them. For these people are the greatest of role models; their struggle and perseverance provide inspiration for us all.

Step 9 helps you get through the adversity in your life. It will help you deal with both events you might have been able to control and those that come as a terrible blow from the hand of fate.

In both cases, the critical question is not, "Why me?" The question is, "How am I going to deal with it?"

Are you going to let adversity stop you and make you settle for less? Are you going to let it stop your dreams? Are you going to let it keep you from reaching your full potential?

Or are you going to learn from it and thus be able to overcome it?

That's the question, and it's essential to being successful at whatever you do.

Adversity requires that you step back and evaluate your role in the situation and determine the lessons you can take away. Only by examining your true value as a person and the strengths you can offer can you begin devising the strategy that ultimately can lead to getting back in the fight.

## ACCEPT RESPONSIBILITY FOR YOUR ACTIONS

To begin, let's talk about situations in which we experience personal or professional failure.

The first step is accepting your role in the failure. You can't blame it all on other people. You can't blame it all on fate. You can't fall victim to the notion that your failure was totally due to forces beyond your control, regardless of what they might be. All this does is reinforce the theory that you have no control over your life and what happens to it, a theory this entire book is trying to debunk.

You create your own luck. You create what happens to you, based on your decisions. You create your future, both by your actions and your nonactions.

But some kind of failure is inevitable. Remember, the best hitters in baseball fail to hit seven out of every ten times they come to the plate. Many of the best home run hitters also strike out a lot. The best salespeople have days when they don't sell anything. Artists have days when nothing creative happens. We all fail sometimes.

The question is what do you do with that failure?

Do you feel sorry for yourself? Do you quit, tell yourself that success is just too hard to work for, a mountain that you can't possibly climb? Or do you simply rededicate yourself, learn from your mistakes, and forge on?

Do you listen to the Fellowship of the Miserable, the ones who will tell you only that you can't do things? Don't, because it's a chorus that eventually will drag you down.

And while there's no question that you may not be able to control all circumstances, it is self-defeating and wrong to blame all failures on circumstances. A serious failure demands serious self-examination.

So every time you fail you have to ask yourself some hard questions.

Did I adequately plan for market changes? Could I have foreseen the ax coming and started working on my résumé a lot sooner? Did I miss the one key point that could have won the case for my client?

In other words, why did I fail? Did I stray too far from my goals? Did I work hard enough? Did I not follow through because I wasn't disciplined and didn't organize my plan of attack? Did my attitude get in the way?

If you can isolate particular points that went wrong with an otherwise good plan of attack, you can separate what you've done well from what you haven't done well. This enables you to keep your self-confidence and not see everything you did as leading up to one big failure. Once you've identified the weak points in your performance, you can stick to the good behaviors you've already learned, get rid of any bad habits or excuses and start moving forward again.

You must also be careful about how you respond to the setback, especially to the people around you.

It's important to avoid placing blame on someone else. This is especially true in a work situation when things are not going well: The company has a setback, everyone's role starts to get questioned, and inevitably the finger-pointing starts, along with the back-stabbing and subsequent low morale. This is the kiss of death, both for you and the group you're a part of.

You must accept both the responsibility and a share of the blame for not succeeding as a group. You must always realize that in any workplace you are part of a collective effort, one in which everyone not only is supposed to be working toward the same mission but also is aware that their individual fate is linked to everyone else.

As a coach I've been involved in several comebacks that have bordered on the improbable, times that we seemed to be facing certain defeat but then went on to win. During the 1993–'94 season, we were down thirty-one points with fifteen minutes left to play at LSU. In an NCAA tournament game, while I was at Providence, we were down ten points with five minutes to play. Both times, we pulled off a victory.

These tough situations have one common denominator: We never pointed fingers at specific players who weren't performing their best. We never started blaming one another.

More important—and this is the lesson here—is that we never gave up on our plan of attack. We never stopped believing. We never quit. All we tried to do in each of these circumstances was to come together and try to find a way to win. We were determined not to lose, to stay together, to rededicate ourselves to the task at hand.

It's the same strategy you should pursue as an individual. You must examine why you failed, accept responsibility for that failure, and rededicate yourself to your plan of attack. You must put that failure behind you and start to move forward.

This cannot be overemphasized. You cannot continue to linger in the failure, whether it's to bemoan your fate, feel sorry for yourself, or feel that this setback is irrevocable. History tells you otherwise. The lives of people who have accomplished great things tell you otherwise. Yes, you've failed. But now the question is very simple and direct: What are you going to do about it?

Wallowing in defeat only prolongs it. Dwelling on it and its repercussions only paralyzes you, leaving you in some terrible limbo. It makes it easy to start saying, "What's the use?" and it creates an environment where failure seems inevitable.

Understanding that you can control how you fail will help you realize that you can control how you succeed.

## STICK TO THE FUNDAMENTALS

There's no question that adversity causes us to start doubting ourselves. You see this with unsuccessful organizations all the time, whether it's a business, a team, a classroom, or even a family. The more trouble that occurs, the more doubt feeds on itself. Eventually, that doubt can become a monster that takes on a life of its own, poisoning everything.

So how do we combat that doubt?

By sticking to our organized plan of attack.

Case in point.

When I first got the job at Kentucky we immediately implemented a high-pressure defense and an up-tempo offense, even though it probably wasn't the best plan for that particular group of players—we only had eight scholarship athletes—because they weren't athletically gifted enough to play that way. But there never was any doubt, confusion, or lack of clarity on the part of our coaching staff about what the plan was going to be. We knew exactly what we wanted to do and how to get it done, and we wanted everyone to be very aware of it, our players included.

There was never any second-guessing in my mind about what we were going to do. We were going to establish our system and then fill in the holes with more talented players, just as soon as we were able to recruit them. Yes, we had some square pegs in some round holes that first year. Yes, it was a real struggle, both for the players and the coaches. But we succeeded, and we did so because we made repetition and consistency the staples of our program.

The players that we had that first year performed as best they could within our system. Then the following year, the players who returned were better, and we also had brought in some new players who were quicker, taller, more athletic. Each year the system became more refined and the players grew more comfortable with it. It helped our players develop self-confidence as well as a thorough understanding of what we were doing, both offensively and defensively.

The point is that we never doubted our plan. We never panicked. We never set up a time limit. We had patience. We had faith that our plan was a good one, based on proper techniques. We believed in a system, and we had the conviction to stick with it.

Sure, there are times when subtle change is necessary. Sometimes you need to take on different roles. Sometimes you must reassess specific aspects of your strategy.

Unfortunately, most of the time, the first thing a person does when suddenly confronted with adversity is decide he or she has to make sweeping changes. Things aren't working.

Doubt has become a factor. Panic starts to set in. Change starts to look good.

But remember that change can be disruptive, too. Change for the sake of change not only creates doubt and uncertainty but also creates a situation that is constantly in flux. Too much change breeds inconsistency.

You often see this in organizations. As soon as they face tough times they start to doubt themselves and begin to experiment too drastically. What made them successful in the past often gets thrown out as they search for new methods, whether it's their core product, or people, or systems. They not only lose faith in themselves but also lose faith in the plan that made them successful in the first place.

It's the same thing with individuals. Failure leads people to doubt themselves and their abilities. That doubt often leads to a questioning of their plan of action and then to the inevitable slide.

But especially during a period of adversity, your fundamentals become more important than ever. The building blocks that you have worked so hard to achieve are ones you must believe in like never before. Your core behaviors will guide you out of your malaise and get you rerouted onto the right path. It's like the golfer who is going through a bad stretch. The best thing she can do is get herself to the practice tee and go over the mechanics of her swing, making sure she's doing everything right and hasn't inadvertently gotten into some bad habits.

Whenever you are in a slump of any kind, you must get back to your basics. It's like a shooter in basketball.

Let's look at two different scenarios:

In the first one, the player makes a couple of easy, high-percentage shots early in the game. Then he makes two free throws. Then another high-percentage shot. So at half-time he feels good about himself. He comes into the locker room and says how he's in the zone tonight, his shot is falling.

In scenario 2, in the second half of the game the same player takes two long-distance shots early on. Both are low-percentage shots, and he misses them both. All of a sudden he starts to press a little bit, telling himself that his shot is not really falling tonight and that he'll try a few more from the same distance. Then he misses a couple of similar shots, and tells himself he's in a slump.

Is he?

Not really. But by getting away from his basics, he allows himself to get in an unsuccessful situation.

So now he must come back to practice the next day and get back to his basics, and often the supposed slump will quickly vanish.

Whatever the adversity, you must do the same thing. Re-examine your fundamentals. Go back to the basics. Not only is it taking action, it's taking a positive step. Once again, you are beginning to control the situation rather than being a victim of it. You are going back to your organized plan of attack.

Remember, repetition is the key to overcoming adversity. Repetition, and the knowledge that you are repeating the right habits and the right techniques.

## HAVE FAITH IN YOUR VISION

Two men who have been unwavering in their convictions are Ted Turner and Allen Neuharth.

When each of them announced their plans for a new business venture—Turner to begin an around-the-clock news television station, Neuharth to start a national daily newspaper—people were shoving each other out of the way to be the first to claim that these enterprises would never fly. They both had a multitude of skeptics doubting them at every turn.

But Turner and Neuharth stood firm They ignored the naysayers, that chorus of negative voices, even during those first years when both CNN and *USA Today* were losing millions of dollars. They did not doubt themselves. They did not panic. They did not let negativity cloud their thinking. They had an absolute, unshakable belief in their visions.

The result?

Both CNN and *USA Today* revolutionized and redefined the news industry.

Why?

Because both Turner and Neuharth were not only men of vision but also were courageous enough to cling to the vision, even in the face of adversity and criticism.

We all know that this isn't easy.

It takes both perseverance and an iron will. Maybe more important, it takes an unyielding belief in your own vision. Because when you fail it's often not the inherent goal that was wrong or misguided, it was simply that the means to that goal were inappropriate. You must be able to separate your vision from the path to that vision—sometimes it's just the route you take that has to be altered. If you believe in something, you might have devastating failures on the road to that dream, but you must remember that the most successful people have succeeded by sticking to what they believed in.

Let's examine that further.

Throughout last year I kept reading articles that although I had been to six NCAA tournaments I had never won the title. When is Pitino going to win the big one? *Is* Pitino ever going to win the big one? *Can* Pitino ever win the big one? Even when we had made it all the way to the Final Four in the Meadowlands, people were still asking those questions.

How did I deal with this?

By keeping my vision. By realizing that all I could do was keep doing what I had been doing: trying to recruit the best players possible, trying to get them to play together, trying to get them to play hard, trying to get them to play unselfishly and care about each other. That was all I could do, nothing more. That and believe that if I kept doing all the things I could control—and kept to my vision—eventually we would win. And finally, in 1996, we did.

The point is, you can't listen to the critics. You can't let them affect you. You must ignore their message and be totally convinced that once you've found your motive, established your work ethic, and begun practicing the proper techniques, you are on your way to being more successful. You have to have that belief, and you have to keep acting on it.

This is what overachievers do. They understand that failure is just more fuel, or added experience, that will allow them not to make those same mistakes in the future. They understand that failure is simply part of the process and certainly nothing to get discouraged about. They understand that failure is often not the result of a faulty vision, but that somehow they got off on the wrong path in pursuit of that vision. They understand that scores of people who have gone on to have incredible successes also suffered incredible setbacks and that it is exactly at these times that it's imperative to keep believing in themselves and their organized plan of attack.

## A GOOD LOSER WILL BECOME A WINNER

I also can't stress enough the importance of handling yourself at all times with class and integrity, especially in tough times that truly test everyone and usually bring out our worst instincts. But no matter what your job is, no matter how many successes or failures you have, you must always conduct yourself with the utmost respect. For the image you leave behind today could well determine how you'll do tomorrow. You want that image to be of a positive, honorable person.

Let's return to recruiting for a minute where persistence is so critical to success. In fact, sometimes a difficult loss in recruiting can be tomorrow's victory.

How?

Because that high school coach is so impressed with the way you handled the loss that he hopes that one day you will coach one of his players.

That happened with us at Oak Hill Academy, a Virginia prep school that traditionally has some of the better high school prospects in the country. Over the years we've gotten down to the wire with several of their good players, only to lose them to other schools. Naturally, we were disappointed.

But unlike some schools who knock the player for not choosing them or who badmouth the school the player ended up choosing, we have always tried to handle losing with class and the knowledge that there always will be other recruits, other chances. I believe that Oak Hill's coach saw that. As a result, I believe he wanted to see one of his players go to the University of Kentucky.

And one of them finally did—Ron Mercer. As a freshman, Ron helped lead us to the national championship. If we had reacted negatively when we lost Oak Hill players in the past, there's no question Ron Mercer would not now be at Kentucky.

There is a lesson here, and it transcends basketball. It's certainly a lesson for salespeople who always are being judged, whether they make a sale or not. If they lose a sale and react badly, they usually are burning that bridge forever.

Yet if they handle that loss with class, they almost always will get another opportunity in the future.

You have to understand that you always are under a microscope, regardless of what you're doing. People always are making judgments about you, forming opinions about you based on how they see you react to certain situations—how you win, how you lose.

So always be concerned with tomorrow and its promise. Always stay the course, secure in the knowledge that we are in this for the long haul, and that today's failure—no matter how devastating it seems now—can one day seem very insignificant. Always remember today's failure can be turned into tomorrow's success.

It might take more hard work. It might take even more of an effort. It might take even more of a commitment. But you can do it. Because you are usually only scratching the surface of what your body and mind can accomplish.

## DEALING WITH PERSONAL TRAGEDY

All of us will sooner or later face personal adversities, whether it's the death of a loved one or another catastrophic event in our lives.

At such times, life is as tough as it gets. These parts of life are the toughest any of us face.

Illness, tragedy, and death take us through the entire spectrum of human emotion. They not only make us let go of our dreams but also make us want to give up everything else as well.

How do we overcome personal tragedy and go on?

In the midst of life's most difficult times, the only way to carry on is by being mentally tough.

What is that toughness about?

It's the awareness that everything doesn't always have a solution. Some of life's mysteries are just that, mysteries. There are certain things that simply are unknown to us. Call it fate. Call it a belief in a higher being. Give it any definition you want. But these circumstances eventually touch all of us, and we must be tough enough mentally to withstand them. If you think about it, we really have little choice. We either learn how to overcome life's tragedies or we sink into the blackness of despair.

In 1987, I learned this the hard way.

Ironically, it was a time that should have been one of the most enjoyable in my life. It was my second year at Providence College, and we had become a Cinderella team, coming out of nowhere, to be in a position to get a bid to the NCAA tournament. One day in March, we were on the bus returning to Rhode Island after playing in the Big East tournament in New York City. The NCAA seeding was going to be held at four in the afternoon, and we were all conducting a team pool on which site we would be headed for, all laughing and joking, as happy as we could be.

But personally, it had been a trying year.

Our son Daniel had been born six months earlier with congenital heart problems. He weighed only three pounds at birth and immediately had been taken from a Rhode Island hospital to Children's Hospital in Boston, a place renowned for its expertise in dealing with difficult health problems in babies. Daniel had a number of things wrong, from a hole in his palate, to loss of hearing, to possibly a pinhole in his heart. The doctors were confident they could remedy some of the problems Daniel was facing with minor surgery; however, he had to get up to eight pounds before he could have that surgery.

My wife, Joanne, gave it her all during those times. She

would leave the house at six o'clock every morning, travel over an hour to Children's Hospital and stay until eight o'clock each night, feeding the baby, watching the baby, nurturing the baby, giving Daniel all the love necessary to progress. She did this seven days a week, without a break.

Then after six months, the reward came. Daniel finally reached eight pounds and was able to go home—not with a clean bill of health, but with the hope that all his health problems could be corrected.

The doctors explained to me that I needed to take Joanne away to give her a break; if I didn't, she was simply going to collapse, physically and emotionally. We had a nurse on call and a doctor close by, so she came to New York with me for the Big East tournament. She was on the bus with us as we headed back home.

As we crossed the Connecticut line and came into Rhode Island a state trooper pulled us over. He came onto the bus and asked if I was aboard. It was 4:05 in the afternoon.

"Please come with me to a pay phone," he said to me. "You have to make a call. It's an emergency."

My first thought was that our sports information director was going to tell me who we would be playing in the NCAA tournament. Providence hadn't been selected to the NCAA tournament in ten years and there was a lot of excitement about it.

But the state trooper had said *emergency,* and I could see his hand shaking, so I knew something was wrong. I quickly figured that one of my older kids had had an accident. In all the thoughts swirling through my head it never entered my mind that anything had happened to Daniel.

I made the phone call, realizing as I did that I was calling a hospital, and a lady came on the line and said, "You have to come here right away."

"I can't," I said. "I'm forty minutes away. Please tell me what's wrong."

"I can't tell you on the phone. Please come in."

"Ma'am, don't do this to me."

"Well hold on, and let me get a doctor," she said.

The doctor picked up the phone and reiterated that I had to come to the hospital as soon as possible.

"I need to know what's going on," I said.

"Daniel died," the doctor said.

Joanne saw the look in my eyes and fainted in my arms. It was the lowest point in our lives. We were numb.

We went to the hospital for the last time and saw Daniel lying on an emergency bed. This small, innocent child lying there without life. It was beyond heartbreaking.

After we got home, I was afraid to sleep. I mindlessly watched game tapes all night, removed from the world.

Providence's magic carpet ride through the NCAA tournament that year was a blur to me. I mean, I know what we did. But it's still a vague montage of images and pain. In a sense the games became a sanctuary, a kind of personal life raft where, for a few hours at least, my mind could focus on something else. Joanne didn't go to the first two games in Alabama, staying back home in Rhode Island with her mother instead. But I told her when I returned that if she didn't come with me the next weekend to the tournament I wasn't going either.

Both Joanne and I have religious faith, but how were we ever going to be able to emotionally deal with something as traumatic as this? How we were ever going to be able to get over the grief? How were we ever going to be able to move on with our lives?

For the next three months there was not much to our marriage. There was not much to my being a father. To be frank, there was not much to our family life, period, as we paid little attention to our three older children.

We couldn't understand how God could have allowed this to happen. After Joanne had spent six months of fourteen-hour days, seven days a week, caring for our child; after finally getting our baby back to decent health, how could God do this to us and to Daniel?

Well, God didn't do it. Life did it. Once we began viewing it that way we were finally able to start getting our lives back.

Eventually, we did not look at Daniel's death as a way to blame God or anyone else. There are simply parts of life we can't understand. It wasn't God's fault. It wasn't anyone's fault. It was just the adventure of life being played out. We can't understand why. The why is part of life's mystery. We knew we had to accept this and return to our lives.

So Joanne and I were eventually able to move on by changing our attitude from pointless negativity to appreciation for the good we had. We turned our attention to our three sons and tried to do positive things in Daniel's name. We focused on what we still had, rather than what we had lost. It wasn't easy; there were plenty of setbacks and periods of uncontrollable sadness, and in a sense we never really got over it. But we were able to continue our lives and our responsibilities and our joys by reframing what had happened.

We learned a valuable lesson during that period, one that's been reinforced many times since then.

When my father died six months after Daniel did, I tried to keep the same attitude. I constantly thought about all the things we had done together, concentrated on the fact that for thirty-five years I'd had the greatest dad anyone could have. When I think of him now, I always smile. I don't allow sadness to come into play.

Sure, there are times when you cry over a personal loss

and times when you grieve and times when you feel the absence of loved ones. But you have to focus on how lucky you were to have those people in your life for the time that you did, and you do that by changing your attitude—nothing more.

That's playing the game of life.

That's what mental toughness is about. When it comes to dealing with a personal tragedy, you have a choice. You can either succumb to it and have it drag you down, or you can fight through it and have it make you stronger. It can either cripple you and thwart your dreams or make you realize how precious life is and how you have to both seize the day and treasure the people to whom you are close. You have a choice when it comes to dealing with life. You must remain rock-solid positive. Not because it's necessarily the right way. Because it's the only way.

## Key Points for Step 9

When adversity hits, as you know it will, deal with it head on. You can't run from it. You can't pretend it doesn't exist. You can't ignore it and simply wait for it to go away.

△

Accept adversity for what it is, and start finding ways to confront it. Take immediate action. You must find the solution and go after it with all the vigor you can muster. You must reemphasize your plan of attack. You must become even more positive, for one of the natural by-products of any kind of adversity is negativity. It instantly starts to sneak in. The more you allow negative behavior to linger, the longer you can expect to have adversity continue in your life. Adversity will usually start to resolve itself when you begin to take action.

△

You must accept your role in a failure. Only by doing this honestly can you pinpoint why you failed and isolate what you need to work on to avoid in the future.

△

Be wary of too much change. Stick to your fundamentals, for they are your building blocks, and they become even more essential in times of adversity.

△

Continue to have faith in your vision. Often it's not the goal that was wrong or misguided, it was the means to that goal. You must be able to separate your vision from the path to that vision.

△

When adversity takes the form of a personal tragedy, you must not see your entire life as not worth living. Recognize the value in yourself and in those you love. Seek out hope, not more despair. A personal tragedy is the worst form of adversity, but it, too, can teach you valuable lessons about learning to seize the moment and realizing the importance of the people you love in life.

# THRIVING ON
# TOUGHNESS

Coach Pitino's work ethic was always such a motivation to me because I was always able to see first hand the time and effort he puts in.

The first thing I learned from him was that hard work overcomes a lot of things. That was especially true the first couple of years he was at Kentucky, when the talent just wasn't there, out hard work allowed us to be successful.

I also think his love for the game motivates you to be the best you can be in your own life, because it's so infectious, and it rubs off on all the people around him. It certainly cid on me. When you're around him it's impossible not to feel the same excitement and enthusiasm that he feels.

His personality, and the way he takes care of his players once they're through playing for him, and the way he takes care of his staff and the things he does for them, is something else that motivates you. They work hard for him and he's the first one to go to bat for them, whether it's trying to get them a better job, or something else. And that motivates you because you know that he's taught you the necessary tools.

I know that's true in my case. I worked hard for him and he was the first one to go to bat for me. You know that if you're working under him, or playing for him, that if you do your job, he is going to be there to take care of you. I think that motivates you to be the best you can be.

Every day, when I'm dealing with my own team, I can feel his influence on what I do, and how I treat my players. He is obviously very tough, very demanding, but at the same time he sends all his players a message that he cares about them. I think that's the most important aspect of coaching that I've learned from him: that you can be as tough as you want to be, but when you walk off the floor you've got to have an arm around them, or pat them on the back.

You've got to be there for them when they need you. You've got to show your players you genuinely care about them. Having learned that from Coach Pitino has made me a much better coach.

And being with him, I was exposed to many instances where his ability to motivate lifted the players and the team to levels they probably didn't realize they could reach. Obviously, the LSU game when we were down by thirty-one yet came to win was one of those times. At half-time he was upset, but there was no one in that locker room that didn't believe we could win.

Also, the team that lost to Duke in the NCAA regional tournament final on Christian Laettner's last second shot in 1992, the shot that kept us from going to the Final Four when talent-wise we never should have even been in a regional final. That year he had everyone believing we could win the national championship. There is no way we should have been able to play with Duke that year, but he had everyone believing that we could beat them.

And we should have.

## Jeff Morrow
HEAD COACH AT LOUISVILLE BALLARD HIGH SCHOOL
AND FORMER MANAGER OF THE UNIVERSITY OF KENTUCKY WILDCATS

# STEP 10 SURVIVE SUCCESS

Struggling with adversity might seem to be the toughest challenge in achieving your dreams, but the greatest hurdle you must face, in fact, is surviving success itself.

But isn't success the point? you ask. Isn't this the end of the journey?

After all, this has been one tough trip. You have constantly examined your strengths and weaknesses and built up your self-esteem. You have eliminated distractions and maintained good habits throughout changes all around you. You have adapted and tinkered and reevaluated and stayed at the top of your game. You have worked harder than you have ever worked before. And you've succeeded.

At Kentucky, we finally won the NCAA championship in 1996. In your case, maybe you won the raise and promotion you had been killing yourself for. Or you lost fifty pounds, took ten strokes off your golf game, or got into the best shape you've been in since high school. Or you finally organized your life and began to feel like you were in control of your time, your finances, and your future.

You can sit back and feel good about yourself, right? You have worked hard for this success, and now you have the right to enjoy the fruits of your labors. You can relax. It's over.

Enjoy yourself—you should. But you must remember one thing. Even the most dedicated and hardworking people are tempted by laziness and complacency once they think their work is over.

But work is never "over."

The ten steps in this book are not a journey with an end. They're an ongoing cycle, an opportunity and springboard for continuous success and self-improvement. Overachievers understand that. They know that they can't relax and take it easy at the end of the race, because there's always another race. They know that the people who truly succeed are the ones who have internalized the good habits and have incorporated them into their lives—not as something they try for a while, like some jacket you wear for a few times and soon tire of, but as things that become a part of who they are every day.

And you can get nine-tenths of the way there, but if you can't complete Step 10—learning how to deal with success—then you cannot begin again the cycle that will lead to achievement down the road.

For success isn't without its dangers.

Success can be a minefield, full of hidden obstacles and booby traps just waiting to trip you up. Success never comes sugar coated with guarantees of longevity. A few missteps, a few moments of letting down your guard— this is a poisonous pill that, if swallowed, can turn long-striven-for success into overnight failure.

How does it happen?

It happens when you embrace success itself and forget

the work it took to get you there. When *being* a successful person takes precedence over the great, motivated person you became and who made you successful in the first place. When you begin feeling not just good but lucky. But when living in the mansion becomes more important than the struggle to get there, then you better start looking over your shoulder for failure. Rest assured that it will be lurking somewhere in the vicinity, because you've committed the killer sin of embracing success.

It happens all the time. In business. In sports. In entertainment. And in our personal lives as well.

Look at the person who goes on a diet, absolutely committed to losing ten pounds. So he eats salads instead of hamburgers. He starts taking long walks. He eliminates sweets from his diets. He stops eating junk food. He gets on an exercise routine. He becomes disciplined and committed. He sticks to his plan of attack. Eventually, he loses that ten pounds.

Then what does he do?

He celebrates by going out and having a hot fudge sundae.

A little extreme?

Not really.

We see it all the time. People who have made a great effort to do more with their lives only to virtually throw it all away once they've achieved something significant. No one's immune. It's like the guy who courts a woman for years, then marries her and feels that he doesn't have to make an effort, that the hard part's over.

A few years ago I had a player named John Pelphrey, who had had a great junior year because he had played with an incredible intensity that allowed him to overcome the fact that he didn't have great athletic ability. It had been a kind of redemption year for him, the season that had proven to everyone in his home state of Kentucky that he really was a good player. But the next year he wasn't playing as well.

Why? Now he was content. Now he didn't think he had to play with the same intensity he had played with the year before. Now he played like he had arrived and he didn't have to prove himself any longer. It's human nature and a trap that's very easy to fall into. You strive for something, you achieve it, and now you feel as if you've finally gotten to the very top of the mountain.

So I called John in and told him that in all the films I'd been watching of him there was something noticeably missing from his game that had been there the year before—the same thing that prevents businesspeople, politicians, and all kinds of other people from duplicating great years: He had stopped working as hard as he used to when he was still trying to get to the top. He got comfortable. He didn't have the same intensity. He hadn't learned how to handle success. Once he did, he went on to have a great second half of his senior year.

So why would anyone embrace success when he or she knows it's poisonous?

Why doesn't he or she avoid the same pitfalls that have brought down so many others?

Simple.

The downside of success is like a virus—invisible, insidious, and a master of the sneak attack. Once you begin to legitimately enjoy your accomplishments, you have to make sure that you don't start believing your own press releases.

## SELF-ESTEEM VERSUS SELF-SATISFACTION

As we talked about in the introduction, a lot of people have a false sense of self-esteem. They're the people who are praised and made to feel good but who have not really done anything to earn that praise. It's so symptomatic of the culture: We want everyone to feel happy with himself or herself, so we often lose sight of the fact that if self-esteem hasn't been earned it's essentially meaningless.

There's a difference between a false sense of satisfaction that comes from people telling you that you're great and you're doing well, and the profound sense of true self-esteem that's based on hard work.

But even with people whose sense of self-worth is based on very real and tangible things, there is the tendency to get lazy. Success builds a level of contentment in everybody who has achieved something significant. Suddenly, you are blinded by the bright light of success, whether it's more money, more recognition, more respect by your peers, whatever the standard of measure. Success also makes you feel good about yourself and makes you want to bask in the warm afterglow.

You often find that people start treating you differently. Often, you find yourself surrounded by a growing number of sycophants, people who tell you what they think you want to hear rather than what's really in your best interest. The so-called yes men. In short, you lose touch with yourself, with that inner person who knows the difference between fool's gold and real gold; between false self-esteem, based on people telling you how great you are, and profound self-satisfaction, based on your genuine achievement.

You already are on the first step of how *not* to survive success.

One of the more intriguing aspects of successful people—the sort the media grab hold of—is how they will spend a lifetime working toward their goals, will labor for years and years trying to achieve a certain net worth or win awards or attain a powerful position, and then—after all that striving and all that hard work—lose it all.

They are the "untouchables," the people who believe their success has made them immune to failure. They can be criminals or businesspeople—an Al Capone or Leona Helmsley— who think they're above the law. They can be athletes who think promiscuity and drug use won't sidetrack them from performing their best. They can be people you work with who have risen to the top quickly and then become victims of their own arrogance.

This untouchable attitude also affects companies. It happened in the automobile industry with General Motors, Volkswagen, and many others. It happens in the entertainment industry, where today's hot studio becomes tomorrow's debt-laden disaster. It happens to restaurants, bars, clubs. One day the people are lined up outside the door. The next? You drive by and the place has a different name.

Even the giants of American industry, the blue chip companies, become casualties of success.

Why did IBM go from 120 points on the stock market to a low of 41? Without question, one of the reasons is that IBM embraced what it had. It wasn't ready for the tidal wave of competition led by Microsoft. Instead, IBM thought it had cornered the market in the computer business.

I have no doubt that the people at IBM continued to work hard and were productive. Certainly, they wanted to perform well, and they probably thought that they were. But they had swallowed the poison of embracing the great success they had known for decades. They didn't adapt to change. They weren't ready for the 1990s.

Eventually, IBM had to bring in Lou Gerstner from the outside to head up the company and jump-start IBM so that it could successfully compete both in the 1990s and into the next century. Now IBM is on the rise again, bigger than ever; its people and its stockholders are once again confident, happy, and optimistic.

IBM symbolizes how comfort can lead to arrogance. They forgot the creativity, motivation, and responsiveness that got them to the top in the first place. The banker who expects customers to crawl up to the president and beg for a loan is courting disaster. What that bank president better do is get out from behind her desk, greet those people when they walk in, welcome them to her bank, and thank them for their business. Because if she doesn't treat them fairly and with dignity, that bank across the street will.

I know that as a basketball coach, no matter how successful I am, I must keep recruiting quality players to Kentucky or we simply will not be as good. It's that simple. It doesn't matter that we have a great tradition and great fans. It doesn't matter that we won the national championship last year. I still have to be familiar with who the best high school players in the country are and which ones will best fit into our system at Kentucky, just as I always had to be when I was at the beginning of my coaching career. I still have to go into recruits' homes and try to convince them and their families why they should come to the University of Kentucky, just like I always had to do when I was working for less sought-after teams early on. To think anything else is self-delusion.

This refusal to sit back and rest on our laurels is the reason why my staff and I vowed last spring to work harder on recruiting than ever before. The minute I tell myself I don't have to do this anymore because we've already won a national title is the day when we, as a basketball program, start to slide. The minute I tell myself that I no longer have to work as hard to try to stay on top as I worked during the ride to the top I am in trouble.

Every year I operate on the premise that I have a one-year contract, no matter how long my official contract is with Kentucky. So should you. Essentially make a one-year contract with yourself, because if you operate under the mentality that if you have long-term tenure then you don't care about today. You postpone. You procrastinate. You tell yourself that you will take care of things in the future. You tell yourself there's no urgency.

We often see this in professional sports. The unwritten rule is: don't trade for a player who has a lot of years left on a big contract because as soon as a player signs a long, multi-year contract, you invariably see that dropoff. Instead, you want a player in the last year of his contract, because then you know you're going to get that optimum performance. You're going to get that great effort.

This is a big contrast with Wall Street brokers who are under the gun every day. They don't have the luxury of post-poning things until tomorrow. They have to take care of today. They always have a sense of urgency about them. They know that in their business what they did yesterday is irrelevant; it only matters what they are doing today.

That's what you have to do.

You can't take things for granted. You can't expect that simply because things are going well for you today there's any guarantee about tomorrow.

You have to create that one-year contract with yourself every year. There's no other way. You have to establish that contract with yourself and honor it every day of your life.

## WHAT DID YOU DO RIGHT?

Once you have achieved something significant in your work or your personal life, take inventory.

You must ask yourself, "How did I do it?"

What direct steps did you take that enabled you to reach your goals? Which ones worked the best? What did you do that indirectly influenced your reaching your goals? Did you do anything that was counterproductive?

Only by examining these things can you remember exactly what led directly to your achievement.

This is extremely important for two reasons: (1) It serves to remind you that it wasn't merely luck, or good fortune, that led to your success. It was hard work. (2) More important, it reminds you that hard work pays off.

That's a powerful message to reinforce, especially when you are in the midst of enjoying the benefits of success. But it's a message you should never forget: Hard work pays off.

In essence, this is the underlying theme that runs through all the steps. As I discussed in Step 1, without that great work ethic you are never going to reach your potential. Without that great ethic, odds are you never would have gotten through Steps 2 through 9 to arrive here at Step 10.

So it's surprising how many people forget this once they finally become successes. It's as if they had just woken up after a long sleep and suddenly found themselves in some strange new place, with no memory of how they got there.

I continue to be amazed by how many players become complacent as soon as they start to have some success. One of my players will be on the second team, and he will work incredibly hard in practice, sometimes even fanatically so, to get into that starting five and have his name announced at the start of a game. This is his goal, and he will do just about anything to reach it, pay any price. Often, it's something he's been striving for since he picked up his first basketball. Then he finally gets there. And what happens? He doesn't play as hard in practice anymore. He's become content.

I just don't understand it.

People achieve success. Then they stop working. It's as if success were the kiss of death.

To my mind, it's almost not worth the journey if you are going to let up. It's like finally getting to the mountaintop and then proclaiming, "Let's go downhill." Why would you go through all that hard work and discipline, only to let it slide so quickly?

I've seen it happen just this season with one of my players, Jared Prickett. He had been starting all year; but he began to take his position for granted, and soon he was playing poorly. So I didn't start him against Louisville, our in-state rival and one of our most intense games of the year.

But Jared knew what he had to do to improve. Once he got back into the game he played better than he had all year. He's now playing with great intensity, and seems to jump higher than ever before.

It was obvious that not starting the game motivated him to raise his performance up to another level once he got a chance to play. The lesson? Jared was obviously content to be in the starting lineup; he was so pleased with himself that he became complacent. He might not have understood that at the time. But I know he realized how dangerous contentment can be when I saw his renewed effort once that starting position had been taken away from him.

What you have to do after you've become successful is maintain excellence. You may not be able to work any harder. You may not be able to be more disciplined. But you probably can be more efficient. You can manage your time better. You can learn from any failure you might have along the way. You can implement better methods. You can find more creative ways to do things. You can take the steps necessary not only to maintain your peak performance, but to keep yourself from the almost inevitable bad habits that seem to creep up along the way.

How do you do this?

One way is to keep reminding yourself of your basics. Make sure your work ethic is as strong as it ever was. Rise earlier, stay up later, read more books and magazines. Eliminate more distractions. Make sure that your goals are still demanding and that you are still as true to your methods as you were when you were on your journey toward excellence.

It's imperative, therefore, to write down what made you successful. Write down the how's and why's. Write down the things that worked and the things that didn't. Study them. They are your clues to what you will do in the future. And then find ways to improve. Keep the fundamentals that made you successful; then get creative enough to improve on them and come up with new formulas to make yourself even better at what you do.

## BREAK IT

We've all heard the old adage "If it ain't broke, don't fix it."

Well, don't believe it.

My advice is simple: "If it ain't broke, break it." Then break it again. Keep breaking it.

After we won the national championship I called a meeting of my coaching staff for seven the next morning. I wanted us to discuss why so many great teams after winning a championship seem to have so many unfortunate things happen to them the next year. Certainly some of these are obvious, namely, that when you're the champ everyone comes after you with a real vengeance. Or that very often your team the next year is not quite the same, because some key players have graduated.

But there's something else, too. And after we had studied several different success situations, we all came to the same conclusion: For so many teams, what destroyed so many seasons after a national championship was the tendency to think they were already doing what needed to be done to win next year.

We made up our minds that morning that we were going to do everything in our power to prevent that from happening to us. We vowed to work harder, longer, and with more intensity than ever before. Yes, we were going to remember the thrill of being champions. Yes, we were going to cherish the moment. But under no circumstances were we going to embrace success and fool ourselves into thinking we were perfect.

So maybe I am going to have to change things somewhat, either by setting higher goals, or by making stronger demands on my players. I must do whatever it takes to keep my players hungry, to keep having that PHD attitude I've talked about. The main way I do this is staying hungry and driven myself.

I have to remind myself that I'm no different from anyone else. I'm as capable of losing that drive and hunger as the next person. And once I allow that to happen I'm in for hard times.

Look at what happened with the Boston Celtics, a great example of a sports franchise that lived by the adage "If it ain't broke, don't fix it."

Didn't they realize that their marvelous trio of Larry Bird, Kevin McHale, and Robert Parish would eventually grow old and need to be replaced? Didn't they realize that new blood needed to be injected into the franchise? Didn't they realize that they eventually were going to pay some terrible price for not dealing with these issues?

Obviously not. That lack of insight, coupled with the tragic deaths of Len Bias and Reggie Lewis, is why that franchise is now struggling so much. Nor are the Celtics alone. The New York Yankees and the Green Bay Packers both went through similar situations. They both failed because they stopped trying to be more creative, more innovative. Only when they got hungry again did success return.

No one wanted those championship teams to fall on hard times. No one planned on its happening, and perhaps it wouldn't have if these franchises had followed the idea of "If it ain't broken, break it"—and then make it better.

That's what you must do after you've been successful. Work hard and dream big, then find new methods and new ways to make that dream become a reality again. Keep breaking it. Over and over again.

Look at McDonald's and Nike, two very successful companies. You can tell by their ads that they're always striving to be better, whether it's by being more creative in their advertising or by introducing more products. They're always trying to change the marketplace rather than have the marketplace change them.

That's what we all must do. Keep being creative. Keep trying to be better at what you do. Keep understanding that nothing ever stays the same, including yourself: If you're not getting better, someone else is passing you by.

Obviously, successful companies and successful people with great wealth would never get to the point where they had to declare bankruptcy if they knew that embracing success was causing their downfall. It's not that their failure is caused by stupidity or lack of effort. Extraordinarily successful people are almost always sharp, intelligent people. They wouldn't have been successful in the first place if they weren't.

No, the problem is they lost their focus. They forgot about the small things that are the cornerstones of success.

How can you avoid similar pitfalls?

Always be competing—even if it's just against yourself. Competition is there, regardless of what arena you're playing in. And if you can't win all the time, you can continue to do the things that put you in a situation in which you will be able to win again. That's the key. Since being successful is a relative term and is sometimes subject to circumstances beyond your control, you can't always guarantee you're going to be successful. What you can guarantee, though, is that you always make sure you are giving yourself the chance to be successful. The key points to remember are:

► Enjoy the moment—then move on. It's human nature to embrace success to some degree. Without question, you should celebrate good times and enjoy the fruits of your labors. You should take great pride in your accomplishments. But your celebratory moments should be short lived, and then you must go back to work.

► Stick with your discipline. Sometimes it's easy to cling to the consequences of success and forget the exhausting path that got you there. Remind yourself that the only way you did it was through hard work—and that's the only way you'll do it again.

► Create new goals. You must always be raising the bar. You must always be setting higher standards for yourself. This is what separates the good from the great. This is what highly motivated people do. They refuse to be satisfied. They refuse to believe they've reached their full potential. They always keep thinking they can do more, accomplish more.

Never underestimate your competition. Your competition doesn't go away. If anything, it works harder. You maintain. They work harder. You don't have to be a mathematician to realize that eventually that discrepancy is going to defeat you.

My third year at Boston University, I fell into that trap. We had been successful the first two years with an unbelievable work ethic, but in the third year I relaxed. I wasn't into getting better as much as I was into maintaining. I didn't have the same work effort and I didn't work my team as hard either. I wasn't as demanding, because I thought I already was successful. I had become content. The result? The worst record in my tenure there.

The marketplace is just as ruthless.

Look at pizza, for example. There's always some new company that's promising to bring it to you faster, cheaper, with better ingredients. Look at golf clubs. Every day there seems to be some new idea, some new gimmick.

Consider that a microcosm for life: There's always someone coming at you with a new strategy, always someone trying to take away what you've already achieved. Refuse to take the poison pill of success. As soon as you achieve anything significant immediately look in the mirror and remind yourself that you are going to refuse to swallow that pill. Remind yourself to refuse to hug yourself, refuse to be ordinary. Stay extraordinary by finding new methods and new ways to make your performance even better.

Remember those companies and sports franchises that went from the top to the bottom. Learn why they succeeded and why they failed. History does repeat itself. If it can happen to them, it can happen to you. If you are not prepared, it will happen to you.

Now we've all heard the old adage "It's tough at the top." It's true.

In sports, it's difficult to repeat as a champion because the competition now understands what made you so successful in the first place. They now know your system. They now have the same hunger and drive that you once had. Now, you've become the hunted, not the hunter.

In business, competition seems fiercer than ever in the 1990s. Everybody is being asked to change—yesterday. Companies are streamlining their workforces. People are having to consolidate their efforts, learn new skills, take on new tasks. We are all being asked to adapt, to get better, be more efficient. If we don't, we are going to get left behind.

With that in mind, you must somehow get more creative and better at what you do. If you don't—if change is something you refuse to do because you've been successful and you don't want to disrupt a winning formula—well, just take a look in the mirror. The happy reflection you see won't be there much longer.

You have to create new ideas and stimulating situations for yourself. You have to get more out of yourself by surrounding yourself with new knowledge and new methods that are even better than the ones you implemented a year ago.

Let's examine John Wooden, the legendary UCLA basketball coach, as an example.

When I think of what he was able to accomplish I am overwhelmed. Ten national championships, including one incredible stretch of seven in a row. It's a mind-boggling achievement, one that will never come close to being equaled.

John Wooden never embraced success. He stayed prepared, hungry, and driven, no matter how many championship banners they hung in Pauley Pavilion. It showed not only in how his teams prepared on the court but in his recruiting. He never had lean years in recruiting. He understood why you win. Yes, it's a team concept. But John Wooden also understood that success really starts with quality people on the court. Then he began the development of their skills and their talents that were crucial to winning championship after championship.

That kind of success could only be achieved because he kept going out there year after year with a great work ethic and by recruiting the quality players necessary to build the great teams he put out on the court. Yes, his pressing defense was fundamentally sound. Yes, his concepts and the unselfishness of his team were second to none.

But it's apparent John Wooden never took anything for granted. He didn't sit back and say, "Well, now that we've won all these titles I don't have to hustle in the recruiting wars anymore because the great players will all want to come here now." He never took that approach. Instead, he worked harder and harder every year.

Commit yourself to constant improvement. Never rest on success.

If you truly understand that, you will never allow yesterday's accomplishments to get in the way of tomorrow's goals.

## Key Points for Step 10

There is no end point to your dreams. It's not enough to become successful; the trick is to become more successful every year.

△

The day after you've achieved something great, be prepared for the question, "What have you done for me *lately?*" When you think the journey is over, you've already started to slide. The methods you used to become more successful must always be a part of your life, otherwise you inevitably will start to drift toward the same bad habits that you spent so much time and effort trying to overcome.

△

Never forget what you did right. It's important to carefully examine the steps you took to become more successful. Write them down. You'll be reminded that it wasn't just luck or good fortune that helped you achieve, but hard work and the right methods.

△

Break it. The great ones are always fixing what they do. Keep being creative. Keep trying to get better. Keep realizing that striving for excellence, striving for success, is a never-ending process, something that has no end. Never stand still: If you are not getting better you are almost certainly getting worse.

# NEVER LET SUCCESS
## SABOTAGE YOUR
## DREAMS

Coach Pitino is a great motivator because of his passion and love for what he does. He illustrates this and demonstrates it so well that the players automatically want to play hard for him. They see that he loves what he does so much, and that if he can love it like that, then they should too.

He also is able to sell his system to the players, to the point that they not only totally believe in it, but they want to play that style. That's what makes him a great motivator in basketball, but it carries over to life too. When the team meets for a film session Coach has a knack for being able to relate what's happening basketball-wise to what's happening in life.

In my days of playing for him at Providence College, after having transferred from Indiana, my confidence was shaken a bit. I had known Coach from the Five Star basketball camp and had been very impressed with him as a fourteen-year-old camper. So I was really excited about the opportunity to play for him.

The basketball season is long, and you have a tendency not to be on the top of your game every single day. One day in practice I was playing hard—or so I thought—but to him I was just going through the motions. Also, I had fallen in love with my jump-shot, instead of putting the ball on the floor and doing other things, like being effective at the defensive end of the court. Things he was accustomed to seeing me doing.

Finally, he said, "Delray, I'm tired of your mediocrity today."

And that one word—mediocrity—stuck in my head.

It's something I've never forgotten. Once you make the decision to do something you have to go all out. I hadn't been doing that on that particular day and Coach knew that. But that word got me going. And it still does. Whenever I'm tired, or I'm not doing something as well as I know I'm capable of doing, I think of that one word—mediocrity—and I try harder. Try to do things the way they're supposed to be done.

### Delray Brooks
FORMER PITINO PLAYER, NOW AN ASSISTANT AT
UNIVERSITY OF KENTUCKY

# OVERACHIEVING IN BUSINESS AND LIFE

It's funny how the term "overachieving" often conjures up a negative image: the workaholic who is never satisfied with one success, who is always trying to achieve perfection in every single thing he or she does.

To many people, overachieving is something to be avoided, as though working hard is something you have to do if you're not as talented or as smart or as lucky as other people. Those people who work hard often hear detractors saying, "Why are you staying so late?" or "Can't you just throw something together for the client at the last minute—they'll never notice?" or "Why don't you come out to happy hour with us and relax—after all, you just got a promotion?"

You can see the pattern here.

But, in fact, overachievers embody the essence of success. These are the people we should consider our role models.

Look at Jerry Rice, who has become perhaps the greatest wide receiver in the history of professional football and still maintains an unbelievable work ethic. Look at Billy Donovan, who through his unyielding work ethic and willpower made himself a college basketball star. Look at the novelist Patricia Cornwell, who spent years at the typewriter before she sold her first mystery novel, but who kept working doggedly at her trade until she became one of the hottest writers in the country. Look at the many people around us who refuse to give up in the face of adversity and eventually accomplish what they set out to do through incredible perseverance and desire.

We all know people who are incredibly gifted at what they do, whether it's business, the arts, athletics, or whatever their arena is. We see their performance and assume that high achievement comes so easily to them. We see their winning results and think that we could never even begin to measure up, that these people are infinitely more talented than we are.

What we usually don't see are the endless hours of hard work they put in to make what they do seem so effortless. We see the ballet, not the years of dance class. We see the grace and beauty of the figure skater, not all those early-morning hours at the cold rink. We see the gymnasts in the middle of the Olympic spotlight, not all the times one of them falls off the parallel bars in practice.

We see the product, not the process.

Invariably, that process is a long and grueling one. Invariably, those people who succeed not only have paid a price to reach the heights they've attained, but they also keep paying that price to maintain their level of excellence.

So let's understand what overachieving is.

It's not some guy holding two phones to his ear, someone who is always in a rush, on his way to somewhere else. It's not someone who appears to be heading off in three different directions. That's the confused person, someone who is caught in a maze.

The other myth about overachievers is that they're all the so-called "Type A" personalities. No doubt you've heard this about overachievers. They often are dismissed as simply being driven and obsessed, as if these traits are somehow undesirable.

But overachieving is a positive quality. It also embraces every other quality we've discussed in this book. Overachieving is about making that great effort that we talked about in the introduction. It's about being organized and having a motive and a plan of attack. It's about reaching optimum performance, which is what we should all be striving for. Give me the overachiever and I will show you someone who not only succeeds, but someone whose work ethic and effort are contagious throughout the workplace.

This book's 10 steps have given you a blueprint for becoming that overachiever. Now that we've walked through the steps and have seen where we want to end up, let's go back to remind ourselves of how to begin this cycle of success.

## STEP 1:
## Build Self-esteem

We can't get anywhere without strong self-esteem. But we have to be honest with ourselves about where it comes from.

The important thing to remember is that self-esteem must be earned. You must deserve it, just as you must deserve victory. If the effort is there, plus the discipline to back it up, you will automatically start to feel better about yourself. Believe me, there is nothing better than the feeling you get when you've taken control of a situation. Just by picking up this book, you've decided to take that first step toward improvement, and that's critical.

After all, whether you believe it or not, you do have control over your life. Life is not something that happens to you, something you are powerless to do anything about. You make the choice to succeed or you fail. You decide by your work ethic and your will. And there is no time limit on this. Nor is there any age limit. It is never too late to transform your life and implement the changes that are going to lead you to your dreams.

The option is always there.

## STEP 2 :
# Set Demanding Goals

Dreams are about the big promotion, the nice house, the NCAA championship, the home run. No one fantasizes about doing drill after drill in practice or staying at work all night to finish a project. But this is how we get to our dreams—through the hard work of achieving our goals.

Goals are the individual steps we must take in pursuit of our dreams. You might have big dreams, but you must understand that your long-term successes are a direct result of what you achieve every day. So our goals can't be merely fuzzy wishes or hastily made New Year's resolutions. They are tangible action items to be written down and followed.

A big component of a successful attitude is to recognize weaknesses and confront them. This is one useful way goals come into play; in this case short-term, attainable goals that can ease you through this somewhat painful process. And after you reach these short-term goals, you can begin to create goals that are more demanding.

Don't make the goals unrealistic, though, because if your goals are too difficult, they can become counterproductive. Understand that you are not going to attain all your goals all the time, but the pursuit of them is a step in the right direction and something that should be commended. Small successes breed larger successes. Conquering short-term goals will naturally lead to attaining longer-term goals.

But although you shouldn't set unrealistic goals, you also must be willing to constantly push yourself. Don't be content with small victories. Maintain your excitement by making your victories bigger and bigger. Not that this is always going to be fun. In fact, most of the time it won't be. The key is to fight through the tough times by reminding yourself that if you stay true to the course there will be a big payoff at the end. Always remember to keep your vision of a better future. Attaining your goals changes your behavior, and it is that change in behavior that will ultimately lead to your dreams.

## STEP 3:
## Always Be Positive

You can be extremely hardworking, but if you're not positive, you're inhibiting your chance at success.

The problem is that we are constantly surrounded by naysayers, whether it's family, friends, co-workers, or a cynical culture. It's very frustrating, for these negative voices can become a chorus that knocks the life out of you. You must try to cut these people from your life, or if that's impossible, at least be aware of their destructive message.

The reality is that we can control our mood. Unlike so many other things in life that you can't change, you can control your mood. Moods can be reversed, and you can teach yourself to do that. Looking at a situation positively enhances the quality of your life.

Self-motivated people look at each day as a new opportunity. You can teach yourself to do this, just as you can condition yourself to look at things more positively, whether it's unexpected change or the minor setbacks we all face in life.

The key is to stay positive in tough times. The rule is simple: The more trying the times the more positive you have to be. This is especially true in the workplace where our industries and our companies are going through challenges all the time. We must look at change as possibility, a chance to be more successful. We must learn to maximize the good times and shrink the bad times down as small as we can possibly make them.

We must also learn how to live in and enjoy the present, free from the failures of the past and the anxieties of the future.

### STEP 4:
## Establish Good Habits

We all have habits that we've picked up consciously or subconsciously over the years.

But are they good habits, or are they leading us toward failure?

The trick is to develop good habits—ones based on proper techniques—and master the art of repetition so that these habits become second nature.

The only way we can systematically acquire good habits is by being organized. We start off each day knowing there is a purpose in everything we do. The day is not merely something that just happens to us. It's something we control and shape with our actions. Getting organized will start to put some discipline in our lives, give our day the structure that we all need. If we're not organized, we set ourselves up to be unfocused, to underachieve and ultimately fail, our best intentions shipwrecked on the rocks of distraction and wasted energy.

Do not put things off. Do the more unpleasant things early in the day, thus freeing yourself for what you enjoy doing. Get yourself in shape to be mentally and physically prepared for your day and strive to impress not only the people you are meeting for the first time but also the people you see every day.

Do your homework. There is no such thing as being over-prepared, especially in today's highly competitive market-place where change is occurring at a dizzying pace. If you are committed to a particular profession, you must know everything you can possibly know about that profession. If you're applying for a job, you must know everything there is to know about the company and the people who work for it. You must always operate on the axiom that knowledge is power, and the more knowledge you have about something, the more completely you can control the situation.

## STEP 5:
## Master the Art of Communication

Good skills are essential, and they start with listening. The ability to interact with people in meaningful ways on a daily basis is essential to the long-term relationships we want to build with them and to the impressions those people will have of us. Most of us can instantly improve our communication skills simply by listening more and speaking less.

One thing to avoid is having to be right all the time. Many people make this mistake and in their desire to always be right, they inhibit constructive communication and prevent relationships from developing. Your goal is to communicate better, not to try to win every discussion or treat every conversation as if it's a contest with a winner and a loser.

You also must communicate both your needs and goals to other people so that everyone can benefit from this knowledge. People want to know why they are being asked to do things. They want to feel they are part of the process. So don't let things fester. Confront problems immediately because if they aren't attended to and dealt with, they invariably get worse.

The key is not to burn bridges. You are trying to create allies, not enemies. This is especially important in the workplace, where you never know for whom you may be working in the future.

## STEP 6:
## Learn from Role Models

On the road to success, you're not just learning from your own experiences.

People all around us have things to teach us if only we could be aware of them. We don't always have to be reinventing the wheel. The people we know and work with must be used as resources, or we are shortchanging ourselves.

So we must have role models in life. We must learn from the people who have made the journey before us. Not only can they tell us the pitfalls to avoid, they can show us the way.

The important thing is to select the right role models. We are not looking for people to entertain us—the class clowns. We are not looking for people who make us feel good—the friends who are always singing our praises. Nor are we necessarily looking for people we like or admire from afar. We aren't looking to join fan clubs. We are interested only in identifying traits in others that we can use to make ourselves better. And these people can be found anywhere—friends, family, whoever. The key is to identify the specific traits that we admire—those traits that can make us better—and emulate them.

We also must learn from others' mistakes. Sometimes learning what not to do is more important than learning what to do. Take advantage of the lessons learned by people who have made the journey before you—consider what might have led to failure, as well as what contributed to success.

## STEP 7:
## Thrive on Pressure

As we struggle with our goals, we must differentiate between stress and pressure.

Stress is the enemy. It robs us of our focus and inhibits our performance. Pressure is only a negative if we allow it to be.

Back when we were children, dreaming our big dreams, we all envisioned ourselves performing in the adult world and accomplishing great things. We never thought about pressure.

We never thought about the things we weren't going to be able to do. That's the mental state we have to recapture, that sense of childhood wonder.

There's no question that we all have pressure points in our lives, so we must identify what they are and begin developing strategies to control them. Identifying what is causing the pressure is the first step, because if we don't deal with the source, it will turn into stress and affect our performance. Pressure becomes a negative only when we are ill-prepared to handle it and not ready to perform in a given situation. But if we've taken the steps to anticipate how we can deal with these situations, we can actually turn up the volume of pressure and let it benefit us.

Pressure also can bring out extraordinary accomplishments. It pushes us harder. It focuses our efforts on the important goals. It concentrates our power where it counts.

Apply the pressure, and you can achieve anything.


STEP 8:
## Be Ferociously Persistent


Who is going to succeed and who is going to fail? What does it finally come down to?

Persistence.

More than anything else, it's persistence that keeps us great. It's persistence that keeps us working at our full potential. Anyone can be great for a day, a week, a month. But the people who ultimately will be successful are the ones who understand that success is a long-term commitment, a marathon instead of a sprint.

So you must develop a "PHD" attitude. Poor, hungry, and

driven. The kind of attitude that will never allow you to be content but will always drive you to learn more and be better. It's the kind of attitude that starts with the premise that we always can improve.

You must also understand that you are always going to face difficult times that tax you and challenge you. The key is to keep working as hard as you ever have, because the harder you work, the harder it is to surrender. The other key is to be flexible; when it appears you are getting sidetracked, you've got to adjust your methods.

But the most important thing to remember?

You must never quit.

No matter what, you must never end the pursuit of your dreams. That's what persistence is all about.

## STEP 9:
## Learn from Adversity

Even if some of us are tough enough to power through life's challenges with a seemingly unstoppable attitude, we all at one time or another encounter an adversity that threatens our will to go on. How do we deal with it? Are you going to learn from it, or is it going to thwart your dreams?

The first kind of adversity occurs when you experience a major failure, the kind that can level you and leave you doubting yourself. This is when you have to step back and evaluate your role in the process. Why did you fail? Were your goals wrong, or was it the means you took to those goals? This is an important distinction. You have to examine your role in the failure and accept your share of the blame.

But remember that during trying times it is essential to

stick to your fundamentals. You have to keep clinging to your vision. Sometimes you will find that your goals weren't misguided; it was your approach to them.

Another kind of adversity that strikes us comes from events we can't control—the personal setbacks or tragedies that we must deal with. We must force ourselves to appreciate the good still around us, otherwise the bad will take undue precedence and ruin our lives. There is always a time for hope.

## STEP 10:
## Survive Success

Becoming successful is a process that never ends.

The methods you used to become successful must always be a part of your life, or you will start to drift back to the same bad habits that you put so much time and effort into changing in the first place.

Success comes with no guarantees: Today's success is often tomorrow's failure. A failure to maintain discipline causes it to evaporate immediately.

It's that fragile.

So never forget what you did right. Keep going back and examining what you did to get you here. Write down your own secrets to success. Study them. If nothing else, they will remind you that it wasn't luck or good fortune that caused your success, but an entire lifestyle of achievement.

This 10-step program is not intended to walk you through a linear progression from a beginning to an end. Once you've taken all these steps to success, you are now ready to enter a cycle of success. This is a blueprint for a lifetime, steps to be followed over and over, an ongoing process.

If you think of it that way there is no limit to what you can achieve.

Consider my 1992 Kentucky team, a team that only the year before had been on NCAA probation, a team that featured four senior players—John Pelphrey, Richie Farmer, Deron Feldhaus, and Sean Woods.

These four players had stayed put after Kentucky went on probation, and I arrived to start turning things around. One reason they had stayed, obviously, was because they liked the school itself and wanted to stay with their friends. The other was that no one else really wanted them. They all either had flaws in their games or had athletic limitations. They all knew that once I arrived, I would be trying to recruit better and more talented players.

I can vividly remember the first day I met them. I was saying to myself, you left Patrick Ewing and Mark Jackson for this?

One was a skinny kid with red hair. One was an overweight guy who wanted to talk about fishing. One never looked me in the eye and wanted to leave the meeting. And one was trying to sell me a couple of watches.

But three years later, after the team had been completely transformed, I saw John, Richie, Deron, and Sean in a different light. I knew that our program would get more successful at Kentucky. I knew that we would get better players. But I knew then it would never get any more satisfying than seeing what those kids achieved in their final year. They hadn't quit; they had persevered and, in retrospect, I saw that they had become the cornerstones of what we accomplished at Kentucky. In their senior year, they turned the program around and brought the pride back to the university and the state. They gave more than anyone could have ever asked for.

So there we were against Duke at the Spectrum in Philadelphia. It was the finals of the NCAA East Regionals, and if we won we would go to the Final Four, an incredible accomplishment considering that Kentucky had been in the doghouse just the previous year.

With 2.1 seconds left on the clock we went ahead by one on a Sean Woods shot. It appeared we were about to win and go to the Final Four. Watching the players run to the bench during a time-out, all hugging each other, I felt euphoric. I knew how far those four seniors had come.

It had been an incredible game—many people still think it was one of the best NCAA tournament games ever played. We had been down 12 with eleven minutes to play, but had come back to force the game into overtime. The overtime had gone back and forth. And now it appeared as if we were finally going to win. We really were going to be Cinderella.

Then the clock struck midnight.

Duke inbounded the ball to Christian Laettner, their great All-American, who was standing near our foul line, his back to the basket. He caught the ball and in one motion took a last-second desperation turnaround shot.

You guessed it.

In that split second we had gone from riches to rags.

Moments afterward, I went in the locker room and everyone was crying, really sobbing. At first I said very little. I was trying to think of something, anything, to lift the players' spirits, especially the four seniors.

I began speaking, hoping I could say something that would make them feel better. But any time I mentioned the four seniors and how much they had contributed and meant to us, everyone in the room just cried louder.

Eventually, I simply told them that it was a great game, and the difference was that Duke executed in the last three seconds. I also told them that they deserved to cry and to let it all out. I said that we would talk more the next day.

When I went to meet the press I was in a fog. I was totally incoherent. I spoke to the media, but I didn't really know where I was, or what I said. It had been that crushing a loss.

The next day was different.

I told the team that we were part of a program that had gone from being a cover story in *Sports Illustrated* about Kentucky's shame to being one tick of the clock away from going to the Final Four. Then I talked about the four seniors.

"You changed your bodies," I said, pointing to them. "You changed your work habits. You changed your spirit. And the bottom line is not that you won the Southeastern Conference championship. Or that you became one of the final eight teams in the country. Or even that you lost to Duke in one of the greatest games in NCAA history. The bottom line is that you learned the most valuable lesson in life.

"When you began you didn't believe in yourselves. You didn't believe that you could ever be any different from what you were. But you came full circle. You had a work ethic and a dedication second to none. You went from the depths to the zenith.

"And your real journey begins now."

Then I turned to the rest of the team. "These guys showed you the way," I said. "They showed you how to achieve greatness."

A few days later we had a celebration for the team in Rupp Arena. Over 23,000 people showed up. Some had never been inside Rupp Arena, and they brought cameras to record the moment. Hundreds of flashbulbs went off as the lights were lowered, and the spotlight shone on each player as the team paraded on the floor during introductions.

There were a couple of team awards, and then athletic director C. M. Newton called the four seniors and their families to center court.

"Many have scored more points than you have," he said. "They have won many more individual honors. But no one can match what you've given us by putting your heart into the wearing of the Kentucky jersey. Look to the ceiling."

There in the ceiling, sandwiched between some of the greatest names in the long and great tradition of basketball at the University of Kentucky, hung replicas of the jerseys of John Pelphrey, Sean Woods, Deron Feldhaus, and Richie Farmer. Their jerseys will stay in the rafters of Rupp Arena forever.

And you must understand the significance of that. All of the other players up there in those rafters were All-Americans. There also are some great players in Kentucky history whose jerseys have not been retired yet. Many of Kentucky's all-time greats have to wait years for their numbers to be retired. Yet these four were being retired, and they hadn't even graduated.

"The other players up there are All-Americans," C. M. Newton said. "These players contributed in a different way."

The four seniors were crying. Their families were crying. The people in the crowd were crying. It was one of the most moving experiences of my life.

For these seniors weren't All-Americans. They weren't great gifted athletes. They were four young men who followed all the steps we've talked about in this book. They took a journey to success that everyone can take if they truly want to. These four young men dared to pursue greatness and were willing to do whatever it took to get there. They were terrific overachievers and became the greatest of role models.

Can you do what they did?

Can you transform your life and achieve heights you only fantasized about? Can you reach your dreams?

Yes, you can. You, too, can choose success and make it happen.

And remember, as I said to those four remarkable young men:

Your real journey begins now.